Also available at all good book stores

9781785315466

9781785313929

9781785315602

9781909626355

9781785315459

9781785313318

DUNDEE UNITED
ON THIS DAY

DUNDEE UNITED

ON THIS DAY

HISTORY, FACTS AND FIGURES
FROM EVERY DAY OF THE YEAR

MARK POOLE

First published by Pitch Publishing, 2020

Pitch Publishing
A2 Yeoman Gate
Yeoman Way
Worthing
Sussex
BN13 3QZ
www.pitchpublishing.co.uk
info@pitchpublishing.co.uk

A CIP catalogue record is available for this book
from the British Library.

ISBN 978 1 78531 618 0

Typesetting and origination by Pitch Publishing
Printed and bound in India by Replika Press Pvt. Ltd.

This book is dedicated to Susi and Vita, who've been so supportive while I've been spending so much time researching and writing.

ACKNOWLEDGEMENTS

I would like to thank everyone at Dundee United, the SFA and the British Library who helped me. I'm very grateful to everyone behind the excellent arabarchive website, for all of their links to YouTube highlights, to everyone at Pitch, and, above all, to everyone at the National Library of Scotland for being so helpful and for all of those trolleys full of old copies of *The Courier* and *The Evening Telegraph*.

INTRODUCTION

I've always believed that Dundee United have a much more varied and interesting history than the vast majority of clubs, and leafing through many old copies of *The Courier* and *The Evening Telegraph* as I've researched this book has provided the proof to reinforce my opinion.

It's been a great pleasure, of course, to revisit match reports from the 1980s, when United beat Barcelona, Monaco, Borussia Mönchengladbach and many other big European clubs. Seen from the perspective of 2019, when power in world football is held by an ever-decreasing number of mostly Spanish and English superclubs, those achievements now seem even more remarkable than they did then. But they weren't an illusion. Grace Kelly really did see her team get knocked out of Europe at Tannadice. That's how good United became.

The story of how United grew from their humble and sometimes precarious origins – thanks mostly to Pat Reilly, Jimmy Brownlie and Jimmy Kerr before Jim McLean took their achievements to the next level – is equally fascinating, and the story has continued to develop in the post-McLean years, with some great players, long-overdue Scottish Cup wins, and also, unfortunately, periods of unfulfilled potential.

I've also greatly enjoyed exploring unusual events in the club's history, from bizarre incidents on pre-season tours to flirting with a Brazilian World Cup star and banning players for moving to Glenrothes.

It's been a pleasure to research and write about a club with such a fascinating history, and – like Robbie Neilson said on 26th May 2019 – I'm sure that United will soon be back up where they belong.

Mark Poole

DUNDEE UNITED

ON THIS DAY

JANUARY

THURSDAY 1st JANUARY 2015

A great start to 2015 as United thump Dundee in the new year derby at Tannadice, in front of 13,000 fans. Stuart Armstrong deflects a Chris Erskine shot into the Dundee net in the first minute, and an Erskine strike and a Gary Mackay-Steven double make it 4-1 by half-time. Jaroslaw Fojut and Charlie Telfer add two more in the second half, and the 6-2 final score puts United third in the Premiership, just three points behind Aberdeen and two behind Celtic.

WEDNESDAY 1st JANUARY 1913

Dumbarton are the new year's day visitors at Tannadice, but, although a railway special brings 300 fans through from the west coast, *The Dundee Evening Telegraph* reports that very few of them make it to the game, presumably as a side effect of their new year celebrations. The Dumbarton players, on the other hand, show no sign of any hangover as they start brightly in a match full of chances, but Dundee Hibernian – as the club were called before changing their name to United – come back from 3-1 down to draw 3-3.

THURSDAY 2nd JANUARY 1958

United beat East Stirling 7-0. Jimmy Brown and Wilson Humphries both grab doubles, and Allan Garvie, Willie McDonald and Joe Roy score once each. Twenty-year-old Aberdonian defender Ron Yeats makes his debut in the match. He features prominently for United for four seasons, before, in 1961, he's sold for £30,000 to Liverpool, where he becomes hugely influential and plays over 450 games.

SATURDAY 3rd JANUARY 1981

United beat Kilmarnock 7-0 at home, and receive a standing ovation from their fans at full time. But with the first goal coming after 34 minutes, manager Jim McLean berates some fans for a lack of patience, saying: 'We have a particular section in the crowd which repeatedly gets its priorities wrong. Instead of voicing their support when things weren't going well at 0-0, every conceivable abuse was hurled at certain players... That kind of thing is soul-destroying for the players and myself.' McLean praises the players for 'one of the best hours of enjoyment provided by my side.'

SATURDAY 4th JANUARY 1986

Kevin Gallacher – the grandson of famous Celtic player Patsy Gallacher – scores his first goal for United, in a convincing 4-2 defeat of Celtic. Jim Reynolds in *The Glasgow Herald* describes 19-year-old Gallacher as the most promising newcomer of the season and says that United give Celtic the runaround for the whole of the first half. The result puts the Tangerines above Celtic in the league, close behind top two Hearts and Aberdeen, with games in hand.

FRIDAY 5th JANUARY 2007

Manager Craig Levein makes one of his first signings for United, Jon Daly from Hartlepool. Striker Daly hadn't been able to become a first pick at Hartlepool, or at his previous club, Stockport County, but, after initially struggling with injuries, he goes on to score 73 goals for the Tangerines.

THURSDAY 6th JANUARY 1972

One month after becoming United manager, Jim McLean makes one of his first – and one of his most important – signings, as he secures 15-year-old Dave Narey on a schoolboys form. When McLean asks his coach Gordon Wallace if Narey can tackle, run or head the ball, Wallace answers each question the same way: 'When he feels like it he can'. Narey's apparent effortlessness does him no harm though; he makes over 600 appearances for United and 35 for Scotland.

SATURDAY 7th JANUARY 2012

Johnny Russell scores a hat-trick in the fourth round of the Scottish Cup as United travel to Airdrie – who'd beaten Gala Fairydean 11-0 in the previous round – and score six before the hosts grab two late consolation goals. John Rankin, Scott Robertson and Gary Mackay-Steven are United's other scorers. The win sets up a fifth-round tie against Rangers.

SATURDAY 8th JANUARY 1994

Jerren Nixon makes his Dundee United debut as a substitute, in a convincing 3-0 defeat of Hearts. Manager Ivan Golac half-seriously later declares that talented and popular but inconsistent Trinidadian winger Nixon is worth at least £15m, but he's transferred to FC Zurich for £220,000 in 1995.

TUESDAY 9th JANUARY 1996

United cross Tannadice Street and beat Dundee 2-0, in the First Division, with 21-year-old Robbie Winters scoring both goals in a bad-tempered match. Chic Charnley is sent off, in just his second game for the men in blue, and United's Steven Pressley also sees red. United go top of the table as they chase promotion.

SATURDAY 10th JANUARY 1987

United cut the gap between themselves and league leaders Celtic to three points, beating the Hoops 3-2 at Tannadice, as Iain Ferguson, Kevin Gallacher and Eamonn Bannon each take advantage of lax Celtic defending to score for United.

SUNDAY 11th JANUARY 2009

The Terrors beat Division Three side East Stirling 4-0 away at a wet and windy Ochilview in the Scottish Cup, in Craig Levein's biggest win as United manager. Prince Buaben, Darren Dods and Jon Daly score in the first half, and after the break, 18-year-old Johnny Russell grabs his first goal for United, from the penalty spot after he is brought down.

SATURDAY 12th JANUARY 1952

United beat Forfar 8-1 at Tannadice, with Frank Quinn and Peter McKay each grabbing hat-tricks. The first 25 minutes are goalless and the visitors' centre-forward William Brown misses a good chance to open the scoring before the floodgates open. *The Courier* reports that Forfar goalkeeper Adam Good can't be faulted for any of the Terrors' many goals, while praising the home side's Andy Dunsmore, Neil Fleck and George Cruickshank in particular.

SATURDAY 13th JANUARY 1962

Jim Irvine scores a hat-trick but still ends up on the losing side as United almost complete a remarkable comeback at home against Celtic. The visitors are 3-0 up after 21 minutes, then Irvine fires home from 15 yards, but Celtic add two more to lead 5-1 just after half-time. With 20 minutes left, Irvine scores again, and claims his third three minutes later. Wattie Carlyle grabs United's fourth with ten minutes to go, but the Terrors can't find the equaliser.

Kevin Gallacher had a knack for scoring against his grandad Patsy's team, Celtic

SATURDAY 14th JANUARY 1928

The Courier reports that 'goal scoring, never a very prolific art at Tannadice, seems to be the easiest thing imaginable' as United beat their fellow promotion-chasers Arthurlie 9-2. United's first superstar, Duncan 'Hurricane' Hutchison, gets a hat-trick, while *The Dundee Evening Telegraph* singles out forward Johnny Hart – who scores two and sets up a few more – for praise, and says that the scoreline doesn't flatter the home side.

SATURDAY 15th JANUARY 1983

United's title challenge seems to be in trouble following a disappointing 0-0 draw away to Hibs. The Terrors get lucky when referee Alan Ferguson fails to play advantage and pulls play back for a foul by Dave Narey, when Hibs have the ball in the net. Hamish McAlpine saves a penalty later in the game, before Paul Sturrock hits the post and Alan Rough saves well from Ralph Milne. *The Glasgow Herald* describes United as 'a shadow of the team that had shown so much promise earlier in the season' and the result leaves them five points behind Celtic and three behind Aberdeen in the title race.

SATURDAY 15th JANUARY 1944

United beat Rangers 6-2 at Tannadice in the wartime North Eastern League, even though the home side are without key players, including prolific centre-forward Albert Juliussen, who has to play in an army match. 'Rambler' in *The Dundee Evening Telegraph* praises the whole team, and Jock Wightman, Ernie Hiles and Charlie McGillivray in particular.

SATURDAY 16th JANUARY 1965

Danish striker Finn Døssing grabs a hat-trick and sets up Swedish midfielder Örjan Persson's first United goal as the Terrors beat Hibs 4-3 at Easter Road, with all of United's goals coming in the first half and all of the Hibs goals after the break. Døssing and Persson are part of manager Jerry Kerr's hugely successful plan to recruit players from Scandinavia. Døssing scores 76 goals in 115 appearances for United, and he and Persson are soon joined by Swede Lennart Wing, Norwegian Finn Seemann and Dane Mogens Berg, with United's performances improving significantly with the imports in the team.

SATURDAY 17th JANUARY 1931

Roughly 800 fans turn up at Tannadice for the visit of Nithsdale Wanderers in the first round of the Scottish Cup, and witness United's biggest ever win, as they score 14 without reply. Tim Williamson scores five, Jock Bain grabs a hat-trick, Jackie Kay and Dennis McCallum get two each, and Jimmy Cameron and Bruce Harley add the others. *The Courier* reports that the 'plucky' visitors are hopelessly outclassed and bewildered, as United enter the second round at a 'complacent ambling pace'. United – who are chasing promotion straight back up to the First Division after being relegated the previous summer – lose narrowly to Celtic in the next round.

SATURDAY 17th JANUARY 1976

The United fans barrack Jim McLean as the Tangerines lose 4-1 at home to Motherwell and slip six points from safety in second-bottom place in the first season of the ten-team Premier Division. Motherwell manager Willie McLean – Jim's elder brother – tries to placate the Tannadice fans, and Jim McLean pleads with them not to blame the players, saying: 'Anyone who pays their money to watch is entitled to criticise, and our results recently have certainly justified the criticism. I am the obvious target for the critics and I only hope they confine it to me, and not the players.'

SATURDAY 18th JANUARY 1958

United beat Stenhousemuir 6-1, away, through a Wilson Humphries hat-trick, an Alex Cameron double – his first two goals for the club – and one Willie McDonald goal.

TUESDAY 19th JANUARY 1965

Manager Jerry Kerr adds to his Scandinavian contingent by signing Swedish international Lennart Wing from Örgryte, where he had played alongside Örjan Persson. With Swedish footballers being part-time, Wing also works as a fireman, and has to ask his employers for a leave of absence to join United. United fans vote Wing their player of the year in 1966/67, but in the summer of 1967 the Gothenburg fire brigade tell him that he has to return to his job, so he moves back to Sweden, where he starts playing for Örgryte again.

SATURDAY 20th JANUARY 1990

Kevin Gallacher makes his last appearance for United, in a disappointing 0-0 draw with Dundee in the Cup at a windy Dens Park. Gallacher had long been linked with Celtic, but is sold to Coventry for a reported fee of £900,000. He's a success in the English league and plays 53 times for Scotland. Meanwhile, United beat Dundee in the Cup replay.

SATURDAY 21st JANUARY 1995

Striker Sergio becomes the first Brazilian to play in the Scottish league as he makes his United debut in a 6-1 home defeat of Motherwell, which is surely the club's best performance in a terrible season. Paul Lambert sets up Tommy Coyne to open the scoring for the visitors, but a Sergio pass creates the equaliser for Billy McKinlay, who then scores again, from the penalty spot. Craig Brewster adds United's third, before, with 30 minutes left, Sergio is replaced by Jerren Nixon, who scores two more, sets up the sixth for Christian Dailly and then misses an open goal.

SATURDAY 22nd JANUARY 1938

United – playing in the Second Division at the time – cause an upset by beating Hearts 3-1 in the Scottish Cup. *The Glasgow Herald* say United 'well and truly ousted the mighty men of Tynecastle'. Tommy Adamson, Willie Rumbles and Albert Robertson get United's goals, before the great Tommy Walker misses a penalty for the visitors. The Hearts fans' pain is mitigated slightly by Hibs losing to Edinburgh City on the same day.

SATURDAY 22nd JANUARY 1949

In a match that Jack Harkness in *The Sunday Post* describes as probably the greatest cup tie of all time, Second Division United earn their Terrors nickname when they cause another cup upset, beating Celtic 4-3 at Tannadice. The home side have the ball in the net seven times but three of them are chalked off, with at least one being overturned in mysterious circumstances when a linesman convinces the referee to change his original decision. United repeatedly take the lead – through two Peter McKay goals and one from Jimmy Dickson – but the visitors equalise three times, before George Cruickshank gets the winner.

SATURDAY 23rd JANUARY 1954

United's visit to Motherwell starts well, with a first-minute Andy Tait goal, but the other 89 minutes are disastrous as the Terrors crash to their worst ever defeat, losing 12-1. Wilson Humphries scores six for the home side, John Hunter gets four, and Willie Redpath scores two penalties. Three years later, United sign Humphries, and all is forgiven as he finishes his first season at Tannadice as top scorer, with 27 goals in all competitions.

SATURDAY 23rd JANUARY 2016

A rare ray of light in a terrible season that ends in relegation. On this day United – who started the day 14 points adrift of second-bottom Kilmarnock – beat Killie 5-1 at Tannadice. Teenager Blair Spittal scores twice and sets up goals for Mark Durnan and John Rankin, to make it 4-0 at half-time. Seán Dillon gets the Terrors' fifth, in the second half, before Josh Magennis gets a late consolation goal for the visitors.

SATURDAY 23rd JANUARY 1988

United chairman George Fox confirms that rumours that United are interested in signing Brazilian star Josimar – who was named the best right-back at the 1986 World Cup, where he scored stunning goals against Poland and Northern Ireland – are true. The club have agreed terms with the player's agents, with a fee believed to be roughly £400,000, and Mr Fox says: 'We have the money to buy Josimar. It would be a tremendously exciting signing for us, for the city of Dundee and for Scotland.' But two weeks later he joins Sevilla on loan, with a view to a permanent deal. United may have had a lucky escape, because the Brazilian's time in Spain is not a success.

SATURDAY 24th JANUARY 1925

Aberdeen University visit Tannadice in the first round of the Scottish Cup. The students defend well in a goalless first half, but *The Courier* reports that United score 'almost when and how they liked' in the second half, taking a 5-0 lead, through a Joe O'Kane hat-trick and single strikes from Willie Oswald and Dave Richards, before the visitors get a consolation goal five minutes before full time.

SATURDAY 25th JANUARY 1913

Dundee Hibs beat Johnstone 7-1. *The Courier* says centre-forward David Scrimgeour is 'eager to a degree' as he scores four, and calls Willie Linn 'nimbleness personified'. Only about 500 fans are present for the game, and one fan writes to *The Courier* lamenting Tannadice attendances and ticket prices, which he thinks are too high for Hibs' predominantly Irish fan base.

SATURDAY 26th JANUARY 1963

One of the worst winters on record devastates the football calendar. On this day, United play their only home match in two months. The game – against Albion Rovers in the Scottish Cup – only goes ahead because the club use tar burners to melt the thick ice from the pitch, which they then have to cover in large quantities of sand. United win 3-0, and performing so well on a desert-like surface leads to the Arabs nickname, which the fans embrace.

SATURDAY 26th JANUARY 1918

Dundee Hibs beat Dundee for the first time, 2-1 at Dens Park, in the wartime Eastern League, in the first season during which both Dundee clubs play in the same division.

SATURDAY 27th JANUARY 1951

With United playing in Division B while Dundee are near the top of Division A, a record crowd for a Dundee derby, of 38,000, squeeze into Dens Park and see the rivals draw 2-2 in the Cup. *The Courier*'s Colin Glen reports that Dundee's opening goal comes from a 'mystifying' penalty award. The home side lead 2-0 at half-time, but United dominate the second half, and goals from Peter McKay and Andy Dunsmore earn a replay.

SATURDAY 28th JANUARY 1967

On the day when Berwick Rangers knock Glasgow Rangers out of the Cup, Dundee United beat Hearts 3-0 in the same competition, at the start of their journey to the semi-final. Finn Døssing scores twice, his first from a poor back-pass and his second from a Billy Hainey ball down the middle, and Finn Seemann sets up Ian Mitchell for the third.

THURSDAY 29th JANUARY 2009

United miss out on a place in the League Cup Final by the narrowest of margins when they lose a record-breaking penalty shoot-out 11-10 to Celtic in the semi-final. Both teams score their first eight penalties, United's Lee Wilkie and Celtic's Glenn Loovens each have their shots saved by goalkeepers Artur Boruc and Lukasz Załuska, and the keepers then each fire a penalty home. With the score tied at 10-10, United's Willo Flood and Celtic's Scott McDonald, who've both already scored, have to take second penalties, but while McDonald scores, Flood – who had a shot well saved by Boruc during the match – hits the bar. Flood joins Celtic the next day, but he doesn't get a chance to prove himself at Parkhead, and he ends up back at United.

WEDNESDAY 30th JANUARY 1980

United beat Dundee 5-1 at home in the Scottish Cup, in front of 22,000 fans, with Willie Pettigrew scoring four and Paul Sturrock one, as Dundee have Stuart MacLaren and Eric Sinclair sent off in the second half. The scoreline would have been even more comprehensive, but Dundee goalie Ally Donaldson saves a Sturrock penalty four minutes after the break. Unfortunately, the Tangerines lose 1-0 away to Rangers in the next round.

SATURDAY 30th JANUARY 1988

United travel to Gayfield to play Arbroath in the Scottish Cup. In his programme notes, the home side's boss John Young says, 'If we play well and United have an off-day, who can tell what the result will be?' Unfortunately for the Red Lichties, the opposite happens, as Alan Irvine scores twice, and Ian Redford, Maurice Malpas, Mixu Paatelainen, Eamonn Bannon and Hamish French grab one each. It's the fifth time that United have won 7-0 under Jim McLean. After the match, Young says that United gave Arbroath 'an object lesson on how to play the game.'

SATURDAY 31st JANUARY 1976

Defender Doug Smith plays his 628th and last game for the Terrors, in a 2-1 defeat away to Celtic. Smith, who often played as captain and was never booked, goes on to become chairman of United.

SATURDAY 31st JANUARY 2015

A strong United side – including Gary Mackay-Steven, Stuart Armstrong, Nadir Çiftçi and David Goodwillie – come from behind to beat Aberdeen 2-1 in the League Cup semi-final, with Çiftçi heading the winner six minutes from time. Unfortunately, Mackay-Steven and Armstrong are both transferred to Celtic after the match.

DUNDEE UNITED

ON THIS DAY

FEBRUARY

MONDAY 1st FEBRUARY 1926

Jimmy Brownlie, United's 40-year-old manager, plays in goal in a Scottish Cup second-round replay against Hearts, with regular goalie Bill Paterson out injured. Brownlie – who had played 16 times in goal for Scotland earlier in his career – concedes six goals, but *The Courier* reports that he 'was by no means a failure. He saved some good shots but was beaten by others that the more youthful Paterson would have stopped.' *The Courier* reserves its greatest criticism for United's forward line, which it says lack 'pep'. The impressive attendance for a Monday match is approximately 20,000.

SATURDAY 2nd FEBRUARY 2013

Jackie McNamara's first game as United manager, against Rangers in the fifth round of the Scottish Cup, gets off to the best possible start when Johnny Russell scores after 14 seconds. With Rangers turning down their ticket allocation because United had opposed their application to return directly to the SPL after they'd gone into administration, only 350 Light Blues fans are among the Tannadice crowd, and their day doesn't get any better, as Jon Daly – who set up the opening goal – doubles the lead, heading home a Willo Flood free kick, and Russell – who also hits the crossbar – gets another, from a Daly pass, near the end, to make the final score 3-0. Rangers' Kal Naismith is sent off for lunging at Flood, and Ian Black is given his marching orders after getting a second yellow card for a foul on John Rankin.

WEDNESDAY 2nd FEBRUARY 2005

United have a nightmare against Rangers in the League Cup semi-final. The Terrors are trailing 2-0 at half-time, before Jason Scotland pulls one back early in the second half, then a Jim McIntyre shot hits both posts and Rangers defender Marvin Andrews seems to handle the ball in the box, but United's penalty claim is turned down. Rangers go on to score five more in the last 25 minutes, through Thomas Buffel, Fernando Ricksen, Nacho Novo and a double from former Tangerines striker Steven Thompson. United boss Ian McCall says, 'The scoreline looks horrendous but for 20 minutes at the start of the second half we had real chances and should have had a penalty.'

MONDAY 3rd FEBRUARY 1936

After drawing twice in the first round of the Scottish Cup, United and Alloa meet for a second replay, at neutral Tynecastle. The Alloa side includes two notable future managers: Bill Shankly up front, and, in defence, Jerry Kerr, who will become Dundee United manager in 1959 and do great things at Tannadice throughout the 1960s. *The Courier* describes the match as a 'hapless display of crudity' but United win 2-1, with a goal from Jimmy Smith and a penalty from Dave Skelligan.

SATURDAY 4th FEBRUARY 1911

Dundee Hibs beat Montrose 6-1 in the Consolation Cup, a short-lived tournament for clubs that had been knocked out of the early stages of qualification for the Scottish Cup. *The Courier* reports that the Hibs are 'much the superior team' and that, in spite of the score, Montrose goalkeeper Paterson 'did a lot of smart saving'.

TUESDAY 5th FEBRUARY 2008

United come from behind at neutral Tynecastle to beat Aberdeen 4-1 in the League Cup semi-final. Andrew Considine gives the Dons an early lead, against the run of play, but Darren Dods knocks home a Christian Kalvenes free kick just four minutes later. Kalvenes gives the Tangerines the lead when he heads home a Craig Conway corner in the second half. Conway adds another, Aberdeen's Lee Miller is sent off, and Morgaro Gomis takes advantage of a short Scott Severin back-pass to add the fourth, setting up a final against Rangers.

SUNDAY 5th FEBRUARY 2012

United beat Rangers 2-0 at Ibrox in the fifth round of the Scottish Cup. An early Johnny Russell goal is ruled out when referee Willie Collum decides that Jon Daly has fouled Rangers goalie Allan McGregor, but Gavin Gunning gives the visitors the lead after just 16 minutes, when he heads home from a Gary Mackay-Steven cross. Mackay-Steven is also involved in the build-up to United's second, playing a one-two with Paul Dixon, who sets up Russell to chip the ball over McGregor and into the net. The win sets up a quarter-final clash with Celtic, which unfortunately goes less well for the Tangerines.

WEDNESDAY 6th FEBRUARY 1946

There's controversy in the Supplementary Cup as United are knocked out on the toss of a coin, after drawing 3-3 with Raith Rovers in a replay. With the score level, the team that earns the most corners would go through, but the sides are also tied on that. So the referee, Mr Blues from Glasgow, tosses a coin and Raith captain McNaught calls it correctly. But United manager Willie MacFadyen protests that the clubs should have first been asked whether they would prefer another replay. League secretary Mr McAndrew is phoned, and he rules that Mr Blues' decision should stand.

TUESDAY 7th FEBRUARY 1995

In the first ever Scottish Cup tie at Broadwood stadium, United beat Clyde 5-1, in a replay after drawing 0-0 at Tannadice. Billy McKinlay opens the scoring, David Craig gets his only ever goal for United and sets David Hannah up for the Terrors' third, before Dave Bowman cracks home his first goal of the season, from the edge of the box, after playing a nice one-two with Dragutin Ristić. And then Jerren Nixon, who's not 100% fit, comes on as a substitute and scores his last ever goal for United, running 30 yards with the ball, beating several defenders and slotting the ball past goalie Les Fridge, to set up a fourth-round tie against Huntly.

SATURDAY 8th FEBRUARY 1913

The Evening Telegraph is full of praise for Dundee Hibs following their first ever Scottish Cup tie, although they lose 4-2 to Queen's Park at Hampden. With 15 minutes to play, Hibs – cheered on by a huge travelling support – are 4-0 down, but then score twice in rapid succession before narrowly missing two more chances. *The Tele* reserves particular praise for 'clever little' inside-left Willie Linn, who 'repeatedly had several of his taller opponents on a string'.

WEDNESDAY 8th FEBRUARY 1967

United travel to Turin for the first leg of their second ever European tie, against Juventus in the Fairs Cup. *The Glasgow Herald* reports that the Terrors 'rarely looked like circumventing Juventus's tight defensive system' as they lose 3-0.

SATURDAY 8th FEBRUARY 1969

Ayr United visit Tannadice in the Scottish Cup. Before the match, Ayr manager Ally McLeod is asked if he'll be happy with a draw, and replies, 'There'll be no draw about it. We're going to win this one.' But the Terrors are 5-0 up after half an hour and go on to win 6-2.

SATURDAY 9th FEBRUARY 1935

United – playing in Division Two at the time – turn in a ruthless second-half performance to beat Division One side Queen's Park 6-3 at Tannadice in the Scottish Cup, with three of their goals coming in four second-half minutes, in front of 21,000 delirious fans. 'The Judge' in *The Courier* doesn't scrimp on the hyperbole, reporting that the best game seen in the city for years 'made old men young and young men younger as they shouted themselves hoarse in that dynamic second half. The full-throated roar, which never seemed to die away for an instant, might have been heard at Hampden… Five wee devils played ducks and drakes with the amateur giants, and each succeeding goal was greeted with a yell and a shower of hats, gloves, and even packs of cards which fluttered down', as the 'bewildered' Glasgow side 'drowned in a goal shower'.

SATURDAY 10th FEBRUARY 1945

United slump to their worst ever home defeat, losing 9-1 to Aberdeen in the wartime North Eastern League. *The Courier* reports that the home side 'seemed blinded by the dazzle of a star-studded team that had perfect movement and a devastating punch', but that United goalie Joe Deans – in his third and final appearance for the club, on a short-term loan from Dunfermline – 'made some dandy saves'.

TUESDAY 11th FEBRUARY 1873

Pat Reilly is born on this day in Dundee. When he's 21, Reilly sets up a successful bike manufacturing business. He goes on to be the key figure in a group of local businessmen who set up Dundee Hibernian Football Club in 1909, and the first manager of the club; and his determination is largely responsible for the club getting into the Scottish League.

SATURDAY 12th FEBRUARY 1977

United win at Ibrox for the first time in 12 years, coming back from 2-0 down to win 3-2, with goals from Paul Sturrock, Gordon Wallace and goalkeeper Hamish McAlpine, who has become United's penalty taker, and scores his third goal from the spot in this match. Jim Reynolds in *The Glasgow Herald* reports that 'United were superb in the second half as they turned on a brand of football that is rarely seen in this country,' and that 'Jim McLean almost allowed himself the luxury of a smile.'

SATURDAY 13th FEBRUARY 1993

Paddy Connolly scores against Partick Thistle at Firhill but, in one of the most unbelievable refereeing mistakes of all time, Les Mottram doesn't award United the goal. The Terrors are leading 1-0, through a first-minute Scott Crabbe penalty, when John Clark flicks on a Michael O'Neill corner and Connolly knocks it home. The United players celebrate, the ball bounces back off the stanchion, and Thistle defender Martin Clark catches it and hands it to his goalkeeper. But, while the happy United players start heading back to their own half, Mr Mottram inexplicably waves play on. Not only has he somehow missed the clear goal, but he hasn't awarded a penalty for Clark holding the ball. The Tangerines players are angry and Jim McLean confronts the hapless whistler, but no goal is given. In the end, it doesn't matter, because the Terrors win 4-0, with Connolly getting two of them. Meanwhile, FIFA select Mr Mottram to be one of the referees at the 1994 World Cup, before, shortly after, outlawing stanchions.

TUESDAY 14th FEBRUARY 1984

United draw 1-1 with Rangers in a fog-enshrouded League Cup semi-final first leg at Tannadice. The fog's so bad that Jim McLean apologises to Arabs fans because they can't see United's goal, which Davie Dodds scores in front of the away fans, but can see Rangers' equaliser, in the same half. No love is lost in the match, with frequent fouls and several bookings. McLean complains that too many of the Terrors' matches are run by west coast officials; comments that land him in trouble with the SFA. Unfortunately, the Tangerines lose the second leg.

Hamish McAlpine, the big goalie with a habit of scoring from the spot

MONDAY 15th FEBRUARY 1999

The Evening Telegraph holds a telephone poll to gauge the appetite for a merger of the two Dundee clubs. More than 2,600 people phone in, with 58% of callers in favour of amalgamation, a result that surprises many people. Dundee chief executive Peter Marr welcomes the result, saying: 'We are all Dundonians but we are battling against each other to achieve the same thing and to me that is quite silly.' Meanwhile, a United spokesman just says that the results make 'very interesting reading' for both clubs. Representatives of fan groups for both clubs voice their opposition to merger proposals, saying that the poll results are very different to the opinions of the fans who they speak to at games. And shortly after, Jim McLean states that – with United having a healthy balance sheet and having spent £7 million on ground improvements – United would only consider a takeover if it's United taking over Dundee.

SATURDAY 16th FEBRUARY 1952

Peter McKay scores his 22nd, 23rd and 24th goals in just 14 games, as he gets a hat-trick for the second match in a row, in United's 6-2 defeat of Kilmarnock, away, while Andy Dunsmore scores twice and Frank Quinn gets one. McKay finishes the season on 36 goals, one of the six years when he's top scorer.

SATURDAY 17th FEBRUARY 1968

United narrowly lose an incredible 11-goal thriller at Tannadice against Hearts in the second round of the Scottish Cup. Hearts have a two-goal lead after 15 minutes, then the Terrors score four in less than 20 minutes – through Davie Wilson, Andy Rolland and an Ian Mitchell double – but the visitors pull one back before half-time, making it 4-3 to United. Early in the second half, Finn Seamann has an opportunity to stretch the lead, but misses a penalty, and Hearts equalise soon after. A Billy Hainey goal puts United back in front, but Hearts equalise again, from the penalty spot, and former United striker Jim Irvine get the winner for the Jam Tarts, five minutes from the end. On the same busy day, on the other side of Tannadice Street, Dundee are also in action at home, where they draw 1-1 with Rangers.

SATURDAY 18th FEBRUARY 2017

The silver lining of playing in the second tier is qualification for the Challenge Cup. On this day, United beat Queen of the South in the Challenge Cup semi-final. The Terrors are 3-0 up at half-time, with the pick of their three goals a Tony Andreu chip from the edge of the box, after Charlie Telfer and Scott Fraser both scored from close range. The Doonhamers dominate the second half though, with Stephen Dobbie pulling one back, before Derek Lyle adds another in injury time. But it's too little too late, and the Tangerines' 3-2 victory sends them into the Challenge Cup Final, against St Mirren, the following month.

SATURDAY 19th FEBRUARY 1972

New boys Archie Knox and George Fleming each score their first goals for United, as the Tangerines come back from 3-1 down, late on, to draw with Clyde at Tannadice. When Fleming pulls one back with 15 minutes to go, *The Evening Telegraph* says that 'boos of disdain became bellows of enthusiasm' as the Terrors find the urgency that they lacked earlier in the game. Then, with time ticking away, United goalie Don Mackay advances almost to the halfway line to take a free kick, with most of his team-mates surrounding the Clyde goal, and, in the 88th minute, Kenny Cameron gets the equaliser.

TUESDAY 20th FEBRUARY 1934

Dundee United directors announce the shocking sad news that the club is withdrawing from the league, without playing their final eight fixtures of the season, due to financial difficulties, with the club reportedly £18,000 in debt and unable to pay the players' wages or the guarantee for their next match, against Albion Rovers.

WEDNESDAY 20th FEBRUARY 1929

United, who are top of Division Two, beat Division One Dundee 1-0 in a Scottish Cup third-round replay at Tannadice. The home side have to soak up a lot of pressure from the visitors, and deal with an injury to Patsy Deuchar, before Geordie Henderson scores the only goal of the game, from a header, 15 minutes before the end, to set up a quarter-final tie with Rangers.

SATURDAY 21st FEBRUARY 1931

United, chasing immediate promotion back to the First Division, beat Brechin 6-0, to put themselves four points behind second-placed Dunfermline, with a game in hand. Under the headline 'A Nippy Display at Tannadice', *The Courier* proclaims that United are of 'real First Division standard', saying that six players – Bill Taylor, George Gardiner, Tim Williamson, Colvin Bennett, Jacky Kay and Jimmy Cameron – would not disgrace any side in the country.

TUESDAY 22nd FEBRUARY 2000

United beat Alloa 4-0 in the Scottish Cup, in Paul Sturrock's joint biggest win as manager. Antoine Preget and Jim Hamilton score within a minute of each other shortly before half-time, and substitute Steven Thompson scores twice in the last ten minutes. His second comes from the penalty spot, after Maurice Malpas takes the ball from Craig Easton, who was going to take the penalty, and hands it to Thompson to give him a chance to boost his confidence. 'When Maurice Malpas tells you to do something, you just do it, because he knows what he's talking about and it was a good shout,' says Easton.

SATURDAY 23rd FEBRUARY 1952

A record crowd of 26,417 turn up at Tannadice to see B-Division United take on A-Division Aberdeen in the Scottish Cup. The match finishes 2-2, with United's goals coming from Peter McKay and George Cruickshank. Aberdeen manager David Halliday admits that his side is lucky to draw, particularly after United's Andy Dunsmore misses a penalty. Among the spectators is ex-Celtic great Patsy Gallacher, who is in Dundee for the wedding of his son, Dundee player Tommy Gallacher. Patsy says the United team 'has a fine balance and a grand forward line of ball players'. Unfortunately, hundreds of fans inside the packed ground can't see the action on the pitch, and leave to go to Dens Park instead, where Dundee are playing Brechin.

SATURDAY 24th FEBRUARY 1934

Four days after withdrawing from the league, Dundee United are saved. George Greig and former Dundee FC director William McIntosh take control of the club, as they invest the money needed to enable United to fulfil the season's remaining fixtures.

TUESDAY 25th FEBRUARY 1997

United beat Hearts at Tannadice in a Scottish Cup fourth round replay. Lars Zetterlund hammers a long shot against the woodwork in the third minute, and the Terrors get the only goal of the game a minute later, when Robbie Winters nods home a powerful Maurice Malpas header from the edge of the box. In the second half, Zetterlund misses a great chance to stretch the lead, after Erik Pedersen and Kjell Olofsson combine to set him up, and in the last minute Sieb Dijkstra saves well from a Dave McPherson header, putting the Tangerines through to a quarter-final against Motherwell.

WEDNESDAY 26th FEBRUARY 1986

United go 16 league matches unbeaten, as they beat Hibs 1-0 at Easter Road, through a spectacular Eamonn Bannon volley. Jim Reynolds in *The Glasgow Herald* reports that United's win is just as emphatic as their 4-0 defeat of the same opposition two weeks earlier. The result leaves United two points behind Hearts at the top of the league, with two games in hand.

SUNDAY 27th FEBRUARY 2005

During a difficult season, United produce one of their best performances of manager Ian McCall's reign, to beat Aberdeen 4-1 in the Scottish Cup quarter-final, at home. United dominate an entertaining match, with their goals coming from a James Grady double and one each for Alan Archibald and Steve Crawford, while Richie Byrne gets the Dons' consolation goal. Aberdeen goalie Ryan Esson makes three good second-half saves, all from strikes by Barry Robson – who'd been involved in the build-up for United's first two goals – to keep the scoreline almost respectable.

SATURDAY 28th FEBRUARY 1914

Dundee Hibs beat Brechin 7-1 at Tannadice in the semi-final of the Forfarshire Cup. Collie Martin scores a hat-trick while Ned MacDonald and Fred Stoessel get two each. *The Courier* says that 'the combination of the Hibs forwards was frequently of a very high order', and that they 'mystified the Brechiners', in a report that also damns the visitors with faint praise, saying that they 'occasionally gave glimpses of more than average ability'.

SATURDAY 29th FEBRUARY 1992

United field an attacking line-up – including Mixu Paatelainen, Darren Jackson, Duncan Ferguson and Victor Ferreyra – against Falkirk, and win 2-1, with both goals coming from Paatelainen. Despite the result, Jim McLean's not happy with his players. He says: 'Before the game I said there was only one tactic: to get the ball to Victor Ferreyra's feet as much as possible around the box. At half-time when we were 2-0 up and should have been three or four, they were told they needed another goal. This they didn't get, and I can't think how many points we've lost this season the same way.'

DUNDEE UNITED

ON THIS DAY

MARCH

THURSDAY 1st MARCH 1934

Five days after United were saved from going out of business, the new directors, William McIntosh and George Greig, who've fired popular but relatively unsuccessful manager Willie Reid, bring back Jimmy Brownlie, who managed the club between 1923 and 1931. *The Courier* reports that the players – who are 'scattered over various districts' – will be brought together for lunch at the Royal British Hotel before the next match, against King's Park in two days' time, with the team selection being 'a last-minute one'.

WEDNESDAY 2nd MARCH 1983

United give themselves a good chance of qualifying for their first ever UEFA Cup semi-final when they lose the first leg of their quarter-final, against Bohemians in Prague, 1-0. Paul Sturrock, whose wife had a baby daughter early in the same day, stands up to some tough tackling, and sets up some good chances for his team-mates, but United can't get an away goal. Nevertheless, Ian Paul in *The Glasgow Herald* – who has particular praise for Derek Stark, Paul Hegarty and Richard Gough – reports that United 'had chances every bit as good, if not better, than the Czechs, who looked weary and worried men at the end.' Jim McLean says he's delighted with the performance but that it's an injustice that United are one goal down.

WEDNESDAY 3rd MARCH 1982

United win the first leg of their first ever UEFA Cup quarter-final, at home, against Radnički Niš. Daves Narey and Dodds score the only two goals of the game, in a three-minute spell near the end of the first half, but a combination of impressive goalkeeping from Zoran Milenković and indifferent finishing from United leaves the Terrors with a job still to do in Niš.

TUESDAY 3rd MARCH 1970

United beat Brechin 10-1 in a Forfarshire Cup mismatch at Tannadice, with Kenny Cameron scoring five for the hosts. Young goalie Hamish McAlpine – who is still Don Mackay's understudy – does have to make two good saves early on, but as the match goes on the Terrors become ever more dominant, with six of their goals coming in the last half-hour.

SATURDAY 3rd MARCH 1934

In their first match after being saved from going out of business and since Jimmy Brownlie returned as manager, United beat King's Park 8-1. Writing in *The Courier*, 'The Judge' confesses that he can't think of a reasonable explanation for the 'almost incredible victory' against a strong side, and puts it down simply to the 'Brownlie factor'. The Judge describes Willie Ouchterlonie – who scores five of United's goals – as a 'human torpedo', says that George Ross's two goals are the highlights of the match, and calls David Laing's solitary goal a 'snorter'.

WEDNESDAY 4th MARCH 1987

A great night for United in Europe as they welcome Gary Lineker, Mark Hughes and their Barcelona team-mates to a full Tannadice for the first leg of the UEFA Cup quarter-final, and beat them 1-0, with the game's only goal coming in the second minute when 20-year-old Kevin Gallacher lobs Andoni Zubizarreta after being set up by Paul Sturrock. Jim Reynolds, in *The Glasgow Herald*, calls United a 'credit to the whole of Scottish football' as they put Terry Venables' men under 'the fiercest of pressure'. With the tie against the Catalan aristocrats – who were in the European Cup Final the year before – finely balanced, Jim McLean says, 'We will definitely cause them problems over there if we show the same self-belief as we did tonight.'

SATURDAY 4th MARCH 2006

David Goodwillie becomes United's youngest ever scorer, at 16 years and 11 months old, when he comes on as a substitute, five minutes from the end, against a strong Hibs side at Easter Road, and scores the consolation goal in a 3-1 defeat.

SATURDAY 4th MARCH 1939

On the day after his 35th birthday, Duncan 'Hurricane' Hutchison scores his 122nd and last goal for United (as well as his 121st and second to last), in a 6-0 demolition of Forfar, near the end of his second spell as a player at Tannadice. Fourteen years later, Hutchison is invited to join the club's board. He briefly becomes chairman in 1963, and remains a director for the rest of his life.

WEDNESDAY 5th MARCH 1947

Playing a home match at Dens Park because of snow at Tannadice, United draw with a strong Rangers side 1-1 in the League Cup quarter-final second leg. There are very strong suspicions of handball against Rangers' opening goal, in a match where the visitors' famous defenders Willie Woodburn, George Young and Jock Shaw have a difficult time. Alex Lister scores the Tannadice men's equaliser. Playing the last 15 minutes with ten men after Bobby Simpson is carried off injured, United almost get the goal they need when Piper MacKay goes past Young, beats Bobby Brown in goal and watches his shot hit the bar. According to *The Courier*, Rangers are undoubtedly lucky to get away without having to play extra time, as they go through on aggregate, having already won the home leg 2-1.

SATURDAY 5th MARCH 1960

With United, St Johnstone, Hamilton Accies and Queen of the South in a four-horse race for two promotion places, the Terrors sign winger Gibby Ormond – the brother of the famous Hibs winger and future Scotland manager Willie – and centre-forward Tommy Campbell, before a key match against Hamilton. Campbell scores a debut hat-trick against the Accies – who have Jim McLean in their team – and Ormond also gets a debut goal, as United win 5-1.

WEDNESDAY 6th MARCH 1929

The Courier says that United 'have perhaps never given a more polished display', as they beat their promotion rivals Albion Rovers 8-1. Duncan 'Hurricane' Hutchison scores four, Geordie Henderson gets a hat-trick and John Bain grabs the other, as the Tannadice men consolidate their position at the top of Division Two.

SATURDAY 7th MARCH 1936

United score four goals in the first 30 minutes, away to Edinburgh City, and go on to beat their hosts 6-3. *The Evening Telegraph* says that 'all of the Tannadice boys were in tip-top form', with Bobby Gardiner – who scores twice – 'the shining light in a team of stars'. Duncan Hutchison also scores twice, and Arthur Milne and John Milne get one each. The result marks the start of an incredible high-scoring run for United.

SATURDAY 7th MARCH 1981

United sweep emphatically into the Scottish Cup semi-final, beating Motherwell 6-1 in the quarter-final. The Terrors score their first four goals – a Davie Dodds hat-trick and a great Paul Sturrock strike – in the first 17 minutes. Gordon Soutar pulls one back for the Steelmen, before Billy Kirkwood and Dave Narey both score in the second half. But not everyone is totally impressed. Jim McLean withholds £20 from each player – one third of their entertainment bonus – saying that they had too many slack moments and are capable of playing much better. Motherwell manager Ally MacLeod says 'it could all have been so different… I really did believe we could win the Cup.' Doug Gillon in *The Glasgow Herald* says the Motherwell defence 'had more holes than Gruyère cheese and was of the same consistency'.

WEDNESDAY 7th MARCH 1984

United's European Cup adventure is finely poised after they lose 2-1 in their quarter-final first leg, against Rapid in Vienna. Derek Stark gives the Terrors the lead with a 25-yard shot, and Hamish McAlpine – despite being the target of fireworks thrown by the home fans – pulls off a series of good saves, including efforts from the great Hans Krankl. But, with just 14 minutes left, Max Hagmayr equalises for the home side, and ten minutes later Zlatko Kranjčar (Niko Kranjčar's dad) grabs a late winner. Rapid coach Otto Barie says his side will go through, as they're 'streets ahead' of the Scots, while Jim McLean praises McAlpine's performance and says: 'We've got to play a lot better at Tannadice, but the away goal and losing by just one gives us a great chance.'

WEDNESDAY 8th MARCH 1967

In front of 28,000 fans, United beat Juventus at home but go out of the Fairs Cup on aggregate. Leading 3-0 from the first leg, the Italians come to defend, and the home side are reduced to shooting from range, until Finn Døssing scores the only goal of the game, nine minutes from the end, hooking the ball over his head, with his back to the goal, and into the net. United miss out on a semi-final tie with Dinamo Zagreb, but finish their first European adventure with immense credit.

SATURDAY 9th MARCH 1940

As United welcome Third Lanark to Tannadice in the Emergency War Cup, a club official tells *The Evening Telegraph*'s Rambler that United face two bad omens: being the 13th name out of the cup draw, and the Second Division championship flag sticking at half-mast when it's unfurled. But Arthur Milne gets a hat-trick, Bobby Gardiner scores twice and Tommy Adamson and future United manager Jerry Kerr grab one apiece, as the home side win 7-1. A Third Lanark official says 'It's a long time since I've seen a team play with such spirit and enthusiasm', and Rambler is full of praise for United's 'midget forwards', saying that Thirds' defenders 'must have had nightmares about elfin figures like Gardiner and Milne skipping about' at their feet.

SUNDAY 9th MARCH 2014

United thump Inverness Caley Thistle 5-0, away, in the Scottish Cup quarter-final. Nadir Çiftçi gets the first two, before Graeme Shinnie brings down Gavin Gunning in the box, and Gunning converts the penalty himself. To make matters worse for the home side, Greg Tansey is sent off for a lunge at Paul Paton, before half-time. Early in the second half, Gary Mackay-Steven makes it four when he picks up a Stuart Armstrong pass, races clear and fires a shot in off the far post. Armstrong makes it five with a header, to complete the biggest win of Jackie McNamara's reign.

SATURDAY 10th MARCH 1934

United's remarkable turnaround under Jimmy Brownlie continues, as they win his second match back in charge, 5-2 against Leith Athletic on a bitterly cold afternoon in Dundee. The home side score twice in the first 11 minutes and lead 4-0 at half-time. The entertainment continues at half-time when a dog gets onto the pitch. Don John, writing in *The Courier*, says: 'That dog should be booked by the management. It kept the crowd entertained for ten minutes. It nosed the ball about with a sure touch that was not equalled in the football feet of a few of the lads who were off for a rest. It did everything but score!' He also has particular praise for two-goal Bobby Gardiner, saying he's 'as cute as a kitten with a ball of wool'.

SATURDAY 11th MARCH 1939

One week after putting six past Forfar, United repeat the trick, against Leith Athletic, on a mudbath pitch in non-stop rain. But the Tannadice goal machine takes its time to hit top gear, only scoring once in the first half, with four goals coming in the last 12 minutes of the game. The impressive Johnny Hutton, playing as a trialist, scores twice, before his brief United career is cut short by being called up for active service. Willie Black also scores twice, but *The Courier* reports that he's 'not impressive', missing 'at least two chances' for each of the goals he scores, while Joe Black is on target once.

SATURDAY 12th MARCH 1983

Six minutes into a dramatic Dundee derby, as the Tangerines chase Aberdeen and Celtic at the top of the league, the Dark Blues' goalie, Bobby Geddes – who's returning from injury – collides with his defender Jim Smith and has to go off with a pulled hamstring and a trapped nerve. Midfielder Bobby Scrimgeour takes over in goal. Richard Gough beats Scrimgeour twice, but an Iain Ferguson penalty, a speculative Albert Kidd shot and a Cammy Fraser scorcher give Dundee a surprise lead, before John Reilly, Paul Hegarty and Davie Dodds make the final score 5-3 to United, leaving the men from Tannadice two points behind Celtic and three behind Aberdeen. After the match, Bobby Scrimgeour says, 'Although I have never played in goal, somebody had to do it.'

TUESDAY 12th MARCH 1974

United beat Dunfermline 4-0 in a Scottish Cup quarter-final replay. George Fleming scores the first two goals, cracking in a shot from 20 yards after Andy Gray flicks on a Hamish McAlpine clearance, and then turning the ball into the net after the Pars keeper saves from a Gray header. In the second half, Jackie Copland fires home the third after making a great run, and Tommy Traynor – who scored the equaliser in the original tie – capitalises on a mix-up in the Dunfermline defence to make it 4-0. *The Glasgow Herald* says that, on this form, the Terrors – who 'demoralised Dunfermline with high speed play which had punch to match' – could well be in line to reach the final for the first time.

SUNDAY 13th MARCH 2011

David Goodwillie scores with an incredible overhead kick in a 2-2 draw with Motherwell in the Scottish Cup. Goodwillie also produces a great save from goalie Darren Randolph, when he makes a jinking run and fires in a low shot from 16 yards, and has a penalty claim turned down after another run. Jon Daly scores United's other goal, to set up a replay.

SATURDAY 14th MARCH 1936

For the second week in a row, United score six, against Cowdenbeath at Tannadice. But, writing in *The Evening Telegraph*, 'Pivot' says that although 'the home team were worthy and decisive winners, the game was by no means one-sided.' He labels Arthur Milne 'personality number one in the home ranks', calling his well-earned hat-trick the 'feature of this timely Tannadice revival', and says that Bobby Gardiner, who scores once, is the brains of the attack. George Ross and John Milne also find the net for United.

SUNDAY 14th MARCH 2010

At Ibrox, United come back from 3-1 down to draw 3-3 with Rangers in the Scottish Cup quarter-final. Andis Shala opens the scoring for the Terrors, before Kris Boyd converts two penalties and Nacho Novo gives the home side a two-goal lead early in the second half. But then a Morgaro Gomis volley deflects off Rangers defender Steven Whittaker and into the net, and Mihael Kovačević heads home the rebound when a Shala header hits the crossbar, to set up a replay at Tannadice a week and a half later.

SUNDAY 15th MARCH 2015

One month after selling Stuart Armstrong and Gary Mackay-Steven to Celtic, all four matches that United play in one month are against Celtic. On this day, the Terrors put up a strong fight in the League Cup Final, denying Celtic space on the ball, but eventually lose 2-0. The first goal comes when Seán Dillon is off the pitch, receiving treatment following a collision with Virgil van Dijk. Dillon is then sent off early in the second half for a careless challenge on Emilio Izaguirre, and James Forrest gets Celtic's second, near the end.

TUESDAY 15th MARCH 1988

United stretch an unbeaten run to 12 matches as they draw 2-2 with Dundee, after extra time, in an action-packed Scottish Cup quarter-final replay played in rain and mud at Tannadice. In the first half, Eamonn Bannon scores both of the Terrors' goals, the first a low drive from 25 yards and the second hooked over his own shoulder, standing with his back to goal while surrounded by defenders. Dundee keeper Tom Carson makes a good save from a fine 35-yard Bannon strike in the second half, and the Dark Blues pull two back and then win the coin toss to decide the venue for the replay.

WEDNESDAY 16th MARCH 1983

Trailing 1-0 from the away leg, United host Bohemians of Prague in the UEFA Cup quarter-final second leg, in front of a capacity crowd. Paul Sturrock passes a late fitness test before the match, and the Terrors dominate, but the Czechs defend deeply for almost the whole game, and their goalkeeper, Zdeněk Hruška, produces a string of quality saves. Halfway through the second half, Jim McLean sends on striker John Reilly for defender Derek Stark, and with ten minutes left he pushes Paul Hegarty forward too, but Hruška pulls off two of his best saves of the match after that, from Davie Dodds and Billy Kirkwood. Bohemians go on to play Anderlecht in the semi-final, while the Tangerines are left to concentrate on the league.

SATURDAY 16th MARCH 1935

United stick eight past Stenhousemuir, as they challenge for promotion, with four games of the season left to play. In an article packed with adjectives including dazzling, magnificent, smashing and whirlwind, 'The Laird', writing in *The Courier*, says, 'I don't remember ever seeing a team so completely masters of a game.' He adds that United looked good enough to get the 11 goals that would have taken their tally for the season so far to 100, and that 'one cannot wish to see better goals than Arthur Milne produced in the scoring of his hat-trick'. Unfortunately, United lose three of their four remaining matches, including one against Stenhousemuir, and miss out on promotion, although they do end up top scorers in the league, on 105 goals.

SUNDAY 16th MARCH 2008

United almost have the League Cup in their grasp – twice – but narrowly miss out in the final, against Rangers. Noel Hunt opens the scoring for the Terrors when he knocks home the rebound after Allan McGregor saves his initial shot. United then have a penalty appeal turned down when Carlos Cuéllar seems to pull back Christian Kalvenes. And with just five minutes left to play Kris Boyd equalises for the Light Blues. In the first half of extra time, Mark De Vries restores United's lead, but again Boyd equalises, with seven minutes left, and the Tangerines lose the penalty shoot-out 3-2.

WEDNESDAY 17th MARCH 1982

United's UEFA Cup run ends controversially in the quarter-finals. The Terrors are defending a 2-0 lead against Radnički Niš from the home leg, and with Dave Narey and Paul Hegarty in control at the back, the first half in Niš ends goalless, in spite of the referee awarding a series of soft free kicks to the home side and ignoring a punch on Paul Sturrock, while the Scottish match commentator reveals that he 'saw the referee being wined and dined last night and he seemed to enjoy it'. But in the second half, substitute Aleksandar Panajotović scores twice to level the tie on aggregate, before, five minutes from the end, Hamish McAlpine punches the ball clear but has a penalty awarded against him as Slavoljub Nikolić collapses after the ball has gone. Branislav Đorđević converts the spot kick, to knock the Tangerines out. Jim McLean says: 'We were pelted with nuts, bolts and money as well as lighted cigarettes but the important thing at the end of the day is that we didn't play. We got caught up in a psychological trap and tried to defend a two-goal lead.'

SATURDAY 17th MARCH 2007

Craig Levein gets his joint biggest win as United manager, as the Tangerines beat big-spending Hearts 4-0 at Tynecastle. All of the goals come in the second half, after the Jam Tarts' Ibrahim Tall and United's David Robertson are sent off for clashing in the first half. Barry Robson gets a hat-trick and Noel Hunt scores the other, firing home a powerful shot from a Steven Robb cross.

Barry Robson, the influential midfielder and captain who scored his fair share too

SATURDAY 18th MARCH 1933

Willie Ouchterlonie and David Laing each get a hat-trick, as United beat King's Park 7-3. *The Courier* reports that 'a weaving run by [Harry] Brant, who tripped over the ball and then recovered to beat four men and supply Ouchterlonie with a made-to-order pass into the goalmouth, was the tit-bit of the match so far as football artistry is concerned', and declares George Gardiner the game's outstanding player.

WEDNESDAY 18th MARCH 1987

Four days after almost being on the receiving end of a giant-killing, when they needed a last-minute penalty to draw with Forfar in the Scottish Cup, United head to Barcelona for their decisive date with Goliath in the second leg of their UEFA Cup quarter-final. Ramón Calderé's deflected shot levels the tie on aggregate, and it looks like the game will go to extra time, until John Clark powers a header past Andoni Zubizarreta with just five minutes left, leaving the Catalan aristocrats needing two goals. But it's United who score again, with an Iain Ferguson header from a Paul Sturrock cross sealing the Terrors' fourth famous victory against Barcelona, and setting up a semi-final against Borussia Mönchengladbach. Jim McLean says, 'Paul Sturrock tore them apart in both games of this quarter-final. Perhaps we needed fresh legs in the second half, but how could I take anyone off? They were all simply magnificent. This is without a doubt our greatest ever night in Europe.' Disappointed Barcelona boss Terry Venables says: 'Considering the opposition left, United could go on and win the UEFA Cup now.'

SATURDAY 19th MARCH 1983

With the dramatic 1982/83 league title race approaching its climax, United know that only a win will do as they visit league leaders Aberdeen. Dave Narey and Paul Hegarty perform brilliantly in defence, while Ralph Milne scores twice in the first half. Gordon Strachan pulls one back from the penalty spot in the second half and then Milne is sent off when he retaliates to repeated fouling from Alex McLeish. But, in a packed, noisy and expectant stadium, ten-man United defend well and survive a couple of scares to hold on to the vital win in this particularly important New Firm derby.

SATURDAY 19th MARCH 1932

United lose a vital relegation battle against Falkirk – who are two points above them – 4-0, leaving them four points adrift with three games left. *The Courier* laments United's poor finishing but says that, in spite of the score, Falkirk don't have 'anything like a walk-over'.

SUNDAY 20th MARCH 1983

Eiji Kawashima is born on this day in Saitama, near Tokyo. He goes on to play in goal in all of Japan's games at the 2010 and 2014 World Cups, before signing for Dundee United late in 2015, on a short-term deal until the end of the season, as the Terrors fight to avoid relegation. Manager Mixu Paatelainen describes the signing as a fantastic coup. Kawashima makes 19 appearances for United and keeps six clean sheets. After leaving Tannadice in the summer of 2016, Kawashima plays in all of Japan's World Cup games again, in 2018.

WEDNESDAY 21st MARCH 1984

On a night that Jim McLean calls one of the greatest in United's history, the Terrors repeat Dundee's trick of reaching the European Cup semi-final at their first attempt. United do that rare thing for Scottish clubs: winning on away goals in Europe, as they beat Rapid Vienna 1-0 at home, through an early Davie Dodds goal, and go through on a 2-2 aggregate score. With such a narrow margin of victory, it's a tense and nervous evening but United march on, on the biggest stage in club football. McLean says, 'It is absolutely unbelievable that so few players have achieved so much,' and adds that the fans' vocal backing is instrumental in the victory.

SATURDAY 22nd MARCH 1997

United go 17 matches unbeaten, as they beat Raith Rovers 2-1 at home. All of the goals come in the second half, with Kjell Olofsson setting up the first when he gets on the end of an Erik Pedersson long ball then crosses towards Robbie Winters, and the ball ends up in the net. And Winters fires home United's second when the Raith keeper can only parry a long-range Maurice Malpas shot, before the visitors get a consolation goal.

SATURDAY 22nd MARCH 1930

As they fight to avoid relegation from Division One, United win a ten-goal thriller against Kilmarnock, played on a Tannadice quagmire. Killie score first but a quick Jacky Kay double makes it 2-1 to United after just ten minutes. The visitors score three more in the first half to go 4-2 up, while Tannadice centre-forward Andy Haddow puts his shoulder out and has to receive treatment on the pitch. In the second half, though, United are playing with the wind at their backs and away from the sun, and, despite his injury, Haddow scores four without reply, to seal a 6-4 victory.

SATURDAY 23rd MARCH 1996

Knowing that goal difference could be important in a promotion race with Dunfermline and St Johnstone, United beat Clydebank 6-0 at Tannadice, with a Craig Brewster hat-trick, two goals from Gary McSwegan and a towering Owen Coyle header. McSwegan almost gets his third and United's seventh late on, when his 35-yard free kick thumps against the crossbar with so much force that it lands near the edge of the penalty box when it bounces back out.

SATURDAY 24th MARCH 1951

Peter McKay scores four goals in United's 10-1 defeat of Alloa, bringing his goalscoring total for the season so far to 37, as he competes with his friend and rival, Brechin City's Dave Paris – who trains alongside him at Tannadice – to score the most goals. But while McKay is scoring four against Alloa, Paris gets five away to Leith Athletic. Meanwhile, back at Tannadice, the other United goalscorers are George Grant, Frank Quinn, Andy Dunsmore, George Cruickshank and full-back Dave Stratton, who gets two from the penalty spot; his only ever goals for United.

SATURDAY 24th MARCH 1962

In their second season back in the top flight, United win at Ibrox in the league for the first time, through a 15th-minute goal from winger Wattie Carlyle. *The Glasgow Herald* describes the Terrors' performance as calm and confident, while the result does Dundee – who are competing with Rangers for the league title – a big favour.

WEDNESDAY 24th MARCH 2010

United dominate their Scottish Cup quarter-final replay against Rangers, and win 1-0 with a late goal, after being repeatedly frustrated in their efforts to open the scoring. Jon Daly tests Allan McGregor early on with a powerful shot, a Mihael Kovačević volley goes narrowly wide, Steven Naismith almost scores an own goal, and United are denied a clear penalty, when Kyle Lafferty stretches to push a Daly header over the bar. Referee Dougie McDonald awards a corner instead of a penalty, waves away the appeals, and books Garry Kenneth for dissent. In the second half David Goodwillie has the ball in the net, but it's ruled out for offside, and McGregor makes another good save from a Daly header. But in the final minute the Tangerines finally make their dominance count, when David Robertson scrambles a loose ball into the goal, to set up a semi-final against Raith Rovers, while also denying the Light Blues the chance to win a treble.

SATURDAY 25th MARCH 1939

East Stirling – who beat Dundee at Dens Park earlier in the season – visit Tannadice and lose 10-0. Willie Black helps himself to five goals, while *The Evening Telegraph* reports that United 'were in dandy fettle', but also, in spite of the scoreline, 'merciful'. Black finishes the season as United's top scorer, with 23 goals.

SATURDAY 25th MARCH 2017

On a sunny day in Motherwell, United win the Challenge Cup for the first time, beating St Mirren 2-1 in the final. Tony Andreu opens the scoring with a great volley but the Terrors' lead just lasts a minute before Rory Loy equalises for the Buddies. Manager Ray McKinnon brings on Thomas Mikkelsen, giving the Tangerines fresh impetus, and the big Dane gets the winner, heading home from a Simon Murray cross. McKinnon says he's delighted and that 'we have won a cup, we have had the experience of dealing with the final and the pressure that goes with it. So that will be good for me and the players for the rest of the season. They should take a lot of confidence from this.' And United lose just once in their last 12 league matches of the season as they reach the promotion play-offs.

SATURDAY 26th MARCH 1977

Big goalie Hamish McAlpine had his fair share of penalty-taking glory, but it doesn't go well for him on this day as United take on Celtic in Glasgow. Going into the game, the Terrors are second to Celtic in the league, and it's looking good when Danny McGrain trips Paul Hegarty, and McAlpine comes up to take the kick. But Celtic keeper Roy Baines, playing the first of a handful of games for the club, pulls off a brilliant save. To cap an uncharacteristically bad day for McAlpine, he later concedes possession from a goal kick and then brings down Johnny Doyle, giving away a penalty, which Ronnie Glavin fires home.

SATURDAY 26th MARCH 1983

United's league title challenge suffers a setback when Hibs visit Tannadice. The visitors take the lead, before Davie Dodds, Ian Britton and Richard Gough each score for the Terrors. The 3-1 half-time lead seems like business as usual, but it all goes a bit wrong in a second half that Jim McLean describes as one of the worst in his time as manager, with teenager Brian Rice particularly impressive for Hibs, as Willie Irvine pulls one back and then Rice gets the equaliser. Hibs boss Pat Stanton admits 'when we were 3-1 down at the interval, I thought there was no way back', while *The Glasgow Herald* predicts that United 'may come to rue the vital point that they allowed to slip away'.

SATURDAY 27th MARCH 1993

A few days after almost scoring his first goal for Scotland, with an overhead kick against Germany, Duncan Ferguson scores his last goal for United – and his 14th of the season – with a towering header against Celtic.

SATURDAY 28th MARCH 1936

For the third match in a row, United score six, as they beat Stenhousemuir 6-1 at home. *The Courier* describes 'mighty atom' Arthur Milne, who gets a hat-trick, as 'quicksilver to a harassed defence', and has special praise for Willie Watson's last-minute goal, as 'the mighty red-head put all he had into a mammoth first-timer which nearly lifted the net from its bearings.'

MONDAY 28th MARCH 1988

The Tangerines visit Dens Park – so often the site of United success in cup competitions – for a second replay of their Scottish Cup quarter-final against Dundee. After 25 minutes, Ian Redford sets up Kevin Gallacher, who bursts forward and fires a low cross to teenage midfielder Joe McLeod, who scores his first goal for United. The Terrors become more dominant in the second half, and have a penalty appeal turned down and a Gallacher goal disallowed, before Redford increases their lead from the spot in the 75th minute, after Dundee midfielder Stuart Rafferty brings down McLeod. Gallacher soon hits the post, before Ian Ferguson fires home a powerful shot ten minutes from the end. Rafferty sparks a brief brawl and is sent off at the end when he kicks Gallacher, but United's 3-0 victory sets up a semi-final against Aberdeen – also at Dens Park.

SATURDAY 29th MARCH 1986

Richard Gough scores the only goal of the game at Dens Park, as United beat Dundee 1-0, with the Tangerines challenging league leaders Hearts for the title, with Aberdeen behind them and Celtic just about in the race.

WEDNESDAY 30th MARCH 1983

A week before his 21st birthday, Richard Gough makes his Scotland debut, playing from the start in a European Championship qualifying match against Switzerland. The Scots get off to a bad start, in a game that they eventually draw 2-2, but *The Glasgow Herald* absolves young debutants Gough and Charlie Nicholas of blame.

WEDNESDAY 30th MARCH 1988

In what *The Glasgow Herald* describes as a 'sparkling display of attacking football', United beat St Mirren 5-1. The Buddies take the lead, on the counter-attack, early on when Paul Chalmers heads past 20-year-old United keeper Alan Main. But it's one-way traffic after that, as Alan Irvine gets the first two league goals of his brief spell at Tannadice, Dave Bowman gets his first goal for the Terrors, and Hamish French and Iain Ferguson score one each, as the Tangerines seal their highest-scoring league win of the season, which lifts them above Dundee and into fifth place in the table.

WEDNESDAY 31st MARCH 1954

Peter McKay signs off from his incredible Tannadice goalscoring career with a hat-trick in his last game for United, before he moves to Burnley. The match, against Albion Rovers, is United's last of the season, and their 6-2 victory – their third consecutive win as they fight to avoid relegation from the B Division – leaves them above Dumbarton, Alloa and Cowdenbeath, who all have games left to play. Between them, the Blue Brazil, the Wasps and the Sons win five of their seven remaining matches, and United finish second from bottom, avoiding relegation on goal average, thanks largely to McKay's 26 goals in the season. United would have gone down if Stranraer had won the C Division south and west section, but they're overtaken at the top of the table near the end of the season, by Rangers and Partick Thistle's reserve sides, who can't be promoted.

DUNDEE UNITED

ON THIS DAY

APRIL

SATURDAY 1st APRIL 1967

For once Dens Park isn't a happy hunting ground for United in a cup competition, as they lose the Scottish Cup semi-final, against Aberdeen, in front of 41,500 fans. The only goal of a tense, defensive match comes in the third minute, when Tommy Miller inexplicably fires into his own net after goalie Sandy Davie drops the ball from a corner. Miller is so dejected at full time that Aberdeen's Jim Storrie – who has his own slice of misfortune in the match when he misses a penalty – Harry Melrose and Francis Munro walk to the pavilion with their arms round him.

MONDAY 1st APRIL 2013

Seventeen-year-old Ryan Gauld scores his first goal for United, to open the scoring, in a 1-1 draw away against St Johnstone in the league. Manager Jackie McNamara says he believes that Gauld has everything – talent and ability – and is exciting to watch, and the youngster goes on to prove himself repeatedly for the Terrors, before earning a transfer to Sporting Lisbon.

SATURDAY 1st APRIL 1995

Billy Kirkwood's first game in charge, against Rangers, gets off to the worst possible start when Gordon Durie scores for the Light Blues after just 12 seconds. And it doesn't get any better seven minutes later, when Alan McLaren blasts the only other goal of the game – a 35-yard free kick – through a weak defensive wall and past goalie Kelham O'Hanlon. The rest of the campaign isn't great under Kirkwood either, although he does turn things round in the following season.

SATURDAY 2nd APRIL 1932

Battling to avoid relegation straight back to Division Two, United start well in a vital match away to Third Lanark, when Jimmy Dyet scores with an accurate, powerful shot in the fourth minute. United's half-backs and full-backs control Thirds' attackers well, until Archie Buchanan is injured ten minutes before half-time, and the home side equalise while he's off the pitch. United reorganise in the second half, so that Buchanan can move to outside-right, but Thirds score three more, and United are relegated, two games before the end of the season.

SATURDAY 2nd APRIL 1983

Chasing Aberdeen and Celtic, United return to form in the league title race, as Rangers are the latest sacrificial lambs to visit Tannadice. Ralph Milne scores one and Paul Sturrock gets two as the Terrors beat the Light Blues 3-1. After the match Jim McLean reveals how he motivated Sturrock: 'I pointed out to Paul that as he has scored 12 goals this season and Davie Dodds has scored 24, that made him only half the player Davie is.' Next up in a compelling three-way title battle: Celtic, away.

WEDNESDAY 3rd APRIL 1940

Arthur Milne scores four, Bobby Gardiner gets three, Johnny Hutton strikes twice and Tommy Dunsmore gets the other, as United beat a Stenhousemuir side – who'd recently defeated Hearts – 10-2 in the wartime Eastern Regional League. 'Rambler', in *The Evening Telegraph*, says that, towards the end, United 'could have done as they liked, but, having secured double figures, seemed content'.

SATURDAY 4th APRIL 1936

Writing in *The Evening Telegraph*, 'Pivot' reports that United fans are showing symptoms of goal lust, as their heroes – who have scored six in each of their previous three games – put eight past Leith Athletic. Arthur Milne gets four of them, taking his total for those four games to 11; he goes on to finish the season on 32 goals from just 27 league games. Pivot calls Milne devastating and says that every day he seems to become more of a 'spring-heeled Jack', and that it would be hard to persuade United fans that there is a better centre-forward in Scotland.

MONDAY 5th APRIL 1971

United stretch their unbeaten record at Dens Park to nine years as they win a dramatic Monday night derby 3-2. Kenny Cameron and Alan Gordon give the Tangerines a 2-0 half-time lead. Jocky Scott scores for Dundee in the second half, before United's Joe Watson hits the woodwork twice and then Alec Reid makes it 3-1. Jim Steele pulls one back for the home side near the end, and then forces a fine save from Hamish McAlpine right on full time.

SATURDAY 5th APRIL 1975

Eighteen-year-old Paul Sturrock scores his first two goals for United, in a 2-2 draw with Rangers at Tannadice. Sturrock is one of four teenagers in the home side, alongside Andy Gray, Dave Narey and Derek Addison. Joe Hamilton in *The Glasgow Herald* praises Sturrock and Gray for their 'sharp raiding' and says that, with such promising young men in the team, United must be optimistic about their prospects in the Premier League.

SATURDAY 5th APRIL 1930

A painful day for United, as they're beaten 6-1 by the only team below them in Division One, St Johnstone, and relegated, with two league games left to play, 12 months after being promoted.

TUESDAY 6th APRIL 1937

A very sad day as Pat Reilly – the most important figure in the creation of Dundee Hibs – dies at the age of 63, from complications arising from pneumonia, at Dundee Royal Infirmary. After stepping down from the board in 1922, he was an ever-present in the Tannadice stands until his last days. *The Evening Telegraph* reports that Reilly's illness is the first to have ever caused him to miss a day's work.

SATURDAY 6th APRIL 1991

Nineteen-year-old Duncan Ferguson, playing his 12th game for United, scores a spectacular volleyed winning goal in the Scottish Cup semi-final, as the Terrors beat St Johnstone 2-1 at neutral East End Park. Ferguson's height and his ball control cause constant problems to the Saints defence, while Jim McLean praises defender Miodrag Krivokapić's performance.

SATURDAY 6th APRIL 1996

United take a big step towards an immediate return to the top flight, as they score six for the second home game in a row, beating Dumbarton 6-1, while their promotion rivals Dunfermline slip up against Hamilton. The Sons take a shock second-minute lead, but Gary McSwegan scores four in the first half, defender Mark Perry stretches the lead, and Craig Brewster gets his 47th and last ever United goal in a competitive match, to put the Tangerines in the promotion race driving seat.

WEDNESDAY 6th APRIL 1983

The latest twist in the 1982/83 title race: Celtic go three points above United and Aberdeen when they beat the Tangerines in a top-of-the-table clash at Parkhead. Both sides have a number of good chances, in what *The Glasgow Herald*'s Ian Paul describes as an exhilarating contest, before the home side capitalise on a rare Paul Hegarty mistake and Frank McGarvey opens the scoring after 60 minutes, before Charlie Nicholas makes it 2-0 20 minutes later. United face another away match against Celtic in just two weeks' time, which McLean calls the Terrors' 'last chance' in the title race.

SATURDAY 7th APRIL 2007

The New Firm share five goals in an incredible opening 17 minutes in a league match at Pittodrie. Jon Daly converts a penalty in the first minute, after Aberdeen's Michael Hart pulls down Collin Samuel. But nine minutes later, the Dons have the lead, as first a Scott Severin shot deflects off Steve Lovell's heel, past Derek Stillie, and then Darren Mackie scores from a penalty. But within seven more minutes, United are in front again. Noel Hunt heads home a Seán Dillon cross, before teenage midfielder Greg Cameron gets his first goal for the Tangerines, cracking a shot in off the underside of the crossbar. The last 73 minutes of the game produce just one more goal, Cameron getting his second – the only other goal he scores for United – when he taps home after a Noel Hunt shot comes back off the post, to make the final score 4-2 to the Terrors.

MONDAY 8th APRIL 1963

United qualify for the Scottish Cup semi-final for the first ever time, when they convincingly beat Queen of the South at the third attempt in the quarter-final. The original tie and the first replay both finished 1-1, and this game, at neutral Ibrox, is goalless at half-time, but in the second half, the Terrors, playing into a strong wind, take control. Jim Irvine opens the scoring in 57 minutes, before Tommy Millar fires past former Scotland keeper George Farm in the Doonhamers' goal. A Dennis Gillespie lob provides the third, and, six minutes from the end, Ian Mitchell makes the final score 4-0.

WEDNESDAY 8th APRIL 1987

United, the last British club competing in Europe in this season, draw 0-0 at home with Borussia Mönchengladbach in the UEFA Cup semi-final first leg. United are disappointing in the first half, when the Germans, who are playing on the break, almost score twice. In the second half United have two goals ruled out for offside, and an Ian Redford shot strikes the post. Despite the result, Jim McLean isn't giving up hope of reaching the final, but says that the team will have to play even better in the away leg than they did when they won in Barcelona in the previous round. With United also looking forward to a Scottish Cup semi-final, McLean says: 'I'm really desperate to win these two trophies, but not for myself. I want to win them for four players in particular. This club has had outstanding contributions this season from Billy Thomson, Dave Narey, Maurice Malpas and Jim McInally, and if any people deserve to end up as winners they certainly do.'

SATURDAY 8th APRIL 1989

United secure their seventh consecutive derby victory – and tenth derby match unbeaten (eleven if you include the Forfashire Cup) – against Dundee. Paul Sturrock – who's been battling injury problems for most of the previous 18 months – scores his 171st and last goal for the Terrors, in his third-last game, and Kevin Gallacher gets the other, lobbing Bobby Geddes from the edge of the box, in a comfortable 2-1 victory. *The Glasgow Herald* reports that the Tangerines are 'streets ahead' of their neighbours from across the road.

SATURDAY 9th APRIL 1927

Nearing the end of their second ever season in Division One, United earn a highly credible 3-3 draw with Celtic – who are challenging for the title – but still seem certain to be relegated. Celtic take the lead, straight from a corner, after 17 minutes, before two Eddie Carroll goals and a James Meagher header give United a 3-1 lead. But Celtic pull two back in the last 20 minutes, before Meagher has a chance to win it for United in the last minute but hits the post. The result leaves the Tannadice men six points away from safety, with three games left to play.

TUESDAY 9th APRIL 1974

United come from behind at Hampden to win a dramatic Scottish Cup semi-final replay against Hearts, and qualify for the final for the first time ever. Hearts lead at half-time through a Donald Ford goal, but in a five-goal second half, George Fleming wins a penalty from an awkward Jim Jeffries tackle, which veteran captain Doug Smith sends past Jim Cruickshank in the Jam Tarts goal. Two minutes later, Graeme Payne collects a loose ball in the box, beats two defenders and scores his first ever United goal, to give the Terrors the lead. Hearts substitute Willie Gibson equalises with a quality goal but, just a minute later, Andy Gray volleys a Pat Gardiner long ball past Cruickshank to restore the Tangerines' lead. Gray later says it's one of the best goals of his career. Five minutes later, and with five minutes left, an Archie Knox goal makes it 4-2. Ian Archer in *The Glasgow Herald* says that United 'improved in the replay. Payne and Gray, forwards short in years but long on ideas, added the light touch. Fleming was the club's best competitor. Elsewhere, they held firm when it mattered most.' United will face Celtic in the final.

SATURDAY 9th APRIL 2005

Trinidad and Tobago international striker Jason Scotland gets the winning goal as United come from behind to beat a strong young Hibs side 2-1 in the Scottish Cup semi-final at Hampden. Derek Riordan gives the Edinburgh side the lead from the penalty spot in the second half, but Barry Robson sets up Jim McIntyre for the equaliser after 73 minutes, and just three minutes later, Scotland – on as a substitute – fires home the winner from 20 yards, to seal the Terrors' place in the final against Celtic. Unfortunately, United lose the final 1-0, despite playing well and almost forcing extra time when Alan Archibald hits the bar from 25 yards late on.

SATURDAY 10th APRIL 1937

United's flag flies at half-mast in tribute to Pat Reilly during their match against St Bernard's, on the day after his funeral, which had a large turnout, at St Joseph's Church in Wilkie's Lane and at Balgay Cemetery on the Friday.

WEDNESDAY 11th APRIL 1984

A packed, noisy Tannadice is the venue for the first leg of United's European Cup semi-final against Roma. After a nervous, goalless first half, United click into gear after the break. The second half is just three minutes old when Paul Sturrock knocks the rebound from an Eamonn Bannon shot to Davie Dodds, who fires a low shot past Franco Tancredi in goal. Ralph Milne and Paul Hegarty come close to extending the Terrors' lead, then Derek Stark beats Tancredi from 30 yards, before the Italian keeper makes a great save from a Hegarty header and the match ends 2-0. It's a great result, and *The Glasgow Herald* reflects the widespread opinion that it gives United a 'magnificent' chance of reaching the final, but warns that the two-goal cushion 'may prove thin in the cauldron of the Olympic Stadium'.

SATURDAY 11th APRIL 1987

The Scottish Cup semi-final is a Dundee derby – in Edinburgh. Both clubs are keen to play the tie in Dundee, and happy to toss a coin to decide the venue, but they're overruled by the SFA. Jim McLean says: 'If I was just a United fan I wouldn't pay the money to go to Edinburgh – I can understand our fans' resentment and I also understand that they can only dig so deep into their pockets,' and the 13,300 attendance is no larger than could be comfortably accommodated at either Tannadice or Dens Park. The fans who travel to Tynecastle are rewarded with a good game though. Iain Ferguson opens the scoring for the Tangerines, but the Dark Blues score twice to lead at half-time, before Ferguson equalises in the second half, and Paul Hegarty wins it for United, with Billy Thomson making some good saves, to send the Terrors into the final.

SUNDAY 11th APRIL 2010

More Scottish Cup semi-final success for United, as they beat First Division Raith Rovers 2-0. David Goodwillie opens the scoring in the first half when he collects a Danny Swanson pass, goes round Raith goalie David McGurn and slots home from a tight angle. The Terrors dominate the second half, and Andy Webster seals the result when his header from a Craig Conway corner beats the keeper.

SATURDAY 11th APRIL 1925

Delighted fans carry manager Jimmy Brownlie onto the Tannadice pitch as United clinch promotion to Division One for the first time by beating East Stirling 2-1, with two games to spare, in Brownlie's second season in charge. Brownlie's decision to make the players full-time seems to be clearly vindicated by earning promotion so quickly. The promotion-winning goals come from centre-forward William Mackie and defender Dave Richards. Writing in *The Courier*, 'Grenadier' says that, with luck, Mackie might have had a handful of goals, while left-half Eddie Gilfeather played the game of his life.

SATURDAY 12th APRIL 2014

Football fans across Scotland take a keen interest in United's Scottish Cup semi-final against Rangers, largely as the first big test of how good this season's Rangers side are. The Light Blues are unbeaten in League One, a couple of seasons after coming back from their financial problems, in League Two, and have former Tannadice star Jon Daly among several players with Premiership experience in their side. But United – who field an attacking line-up including Ryan Gauld, Stuart Armstrong, Gary Mackay-Steven and Nadir Çiftçi – win comfortably, 3-1. With Hampden undergoing redevelopment work for the Glasgow Commonwealth Games, the match takes place at Ibrox, but the Arabs in the stands contribute significantly to the intense atmosphere, as Armstrong, Mackay-Steven and Çiftçi get the goals.

WEDNESDAY 13th APRIL 1988

Jim McLean gets into trouble following a confrontation in a bad-tempered Scottish Cup semi-final replay against Aberdeen at neutral Dens Park: the fifth out of six consecutive matches in the Cup that the Terrors play across the road. The match is drawn 1-1, thanks to fine goals from Charlie Nicholas and Mixu Paatelainen, but it's remembered more for controversy at the end of the first half. Paul Hegarty is sent off for a foul on Nicholas, but McLean, who thinks that Nicholas dived and that Willie Miller influenced the referee, confronts Miller and Nicholas. After the match, McLean says, 'Only [SFA secretary] Ernie Walker can say what he thinks. I cannot make any comment.' The SFA give McLean a three-year touchline ban, and then McLean tells the United board that he's resigning, but they manage to convince him to stay.

MONDAY 13th APRIL 1936

United record their biggest ever league win, beating East Stirling 12-1 in the last game of the season, at the climax of an incredible goalscoring run of 42 goals in six games, which takes their total for the 34-game season to 108. Don John in *The Courier* reports that an accountant would have found it difficult to keep touch with the scoring, on a remarkable Easter Monday afternoon when Duncan Hutchison and Arthur Milne get hat-tricks, there are doubles for George Ross and Jacky Kay, and Doug Anderson and Bobby Gardiner grab one each.

SATURDAY 13th APRIL 1940

United face Airdrie in the semi-final of the Emergency War Cup. United fans serving in the forces in France arrange for a lucky horseshoe to be sent to Tannadice with the message, 'You win the cup and we'll win the war.' Meanwhile, a special train is laid on to take United fans to Easter Road for the game and 'Rambler', writing in *The Evening Telegraph*, says that enough lucky pennies are thrown from the Forth Bridge to sink any German submarines that may have been lurking nearby. The game finishes 0-0, with the replay due four days later.

SATURDAY 13th APRIL 1963

Brother lines up against brother at a windy Hampden Park, in United's first ever Scottish Cup semi-final, with right-back Tommy Millar playing for the Terrors against Rangers centre-forward Jimmy Millar. United play well for much of the first half, with Rangers goalie Billy Ritchie having to make two good saves in the first 20 minutes. But then a Millar scores two quick goals and unfortunately it's Jimmy. United are soon level, through Dennis Gillespie and Ian Mitchell, but Ralph Brand quickly restores Rangers' lead. The first five goals have come in just 12 minutes. And Jimmy Millar – who will join United four years later – completes his hat-trick just before half-time. The wind gets worse in a second half that has just one goal: a 25-yard George McLean strike, five minutes from the end. The 5-2 scoreline isn't the only bad news for United; the SFA fine them £10 for playing in a new all-white strip, rather than their registered black and white hoops.

SATURDAY 14th APRIL 1984

The fans are allowed in for free for United's league match with St Johnstone, three days after the drama of the European Cup semi-final home tie against Roma. The Terrors win 3-0, with the pick of the bunch a spectacular Tommy Coyne overhead kick, but Jim McLean says: 'Apart from three fine goals, the fans got exactly what they paid for.' McLean and Walter Smith then rush straight to Italy, to watch Roma play Juventus, ahead of United's European Cup return leg.

WEDNESDAY 15th APRIL 1981

United come from behind to beat Celtic 3-2 in a dramatic Scottish Cup semi-final replay at Hampden. The Terrors are 1-0 down after five minutes but, within the next five minutes, Paul Sturrock sets up Eamonn Bannon to hammer home the equaliser, before Bannon turns provider for Paul Hegarty – who had to have a late fitness test before the match – to give the Terrors the lead. Davie Provan equalises for Celtic with a powerful 18-yard strike on the stroke of half-time, and the second half is goalless until, 14 minutes from the end, Bannon gets his head to a long free kick and knocks the ball down towards Hegarty, who competes with Celtic defender Mike Conroy for it, and it ends up in the back of the net, sending the Terrors into the final, against Rangers.

SATURDAY 16th APRIL 1955

United beat Arbroath 6-1 in the league. The score is 1-1 early in the second half, but *The Courier* reports that Arbroath's equaliser spurs United to turn on 'a fine brand of teamwork which had the Arbroath defence at sixes and sevens'. Winger Maurice Milne makes his United debut in the match as a trialist. He goes on to play 84 times for the Terrors, scoring 31 goals.

WEDNESDAY 16th APRIL 1958

An embarrassing 7-1 home defeat to Alloa – who are managed by Jerry Kerr – has a particularly shiny silver lining, as Kerr becomes United boss a year later, and soon signs striker Dennis Gillespie, who scored two of those seven goals against United. Kerr and Gillespie are both huge successes for the Terrors.

SATURDAY 16th APRIL 1927

United win an away match for the first time in their second ever season in the top flight, beating Hearts 2-1, but are relegated nevertheless, with two league games left to play. All three goals come in the first 20 minutes, with Willie Welsh getting both for the visitors. *The Courier* reports that 'bottom dogs' United 'were more than a match for their higher placed opponents.'

SATURDAY 16th APRIL 2016

Hibs goalie Conrad Logan repeatedly denies United in the Scottish Cup semi-final. Logan saves twice from Billy Mckay in the first half, then from John Rankin and Henri Anier in extra time, and – after the match finishes 0-0 – from Blair Spittal, and Mckay again, in the penalty shoot-out. During the match, Hibs striker Jason Cummings attempts a Panenka penalty, which drifts embarrassingly over the bar, but the Edinburgh side score all of their first four penalties in the shoot-out, and United are denied a place in the final.

SATURDAY 17th APRIL 1926

In the last home game of their first season in Division One, against St Johnstone, United get their first ever attendance of over 20,000 at Tannadice, when 23,517 turn up. A fair result of 0-0 in the spring sunshine, in a match that's competitive but that lacks much goalmouth incident, safeguards United's place in Division One for another season, with one game left to play.

WEDNESDAY 17th APRIL 1985

United beat Aberdeen 2-1 in a bad-tempered Scottish Cup semi-final replay at neutral Tynecastle, the first time the Dons have lost in the Cup since 1981. Paul Sturrock opens the scoring with a fifth-minute header, Neale Cooper and Davie Dodds are both sent off, and Stuart Beedie scores with a magnificent volley before Ian Angus pulls one back for the Dons, to set up a tense final five minutes, but United stand firm to set up a final against Celtic. 'I think every fan got their money's worth tonight,' says Jim McLean, 'and our second goal was fit to win any match.' In the final, against Celtic, United play well but lose 2-1.

WEDNESDAY 17th APRIL 1940

Stanley Matthews lines up against United, for Airdrie in the Emergency War Cup semi-final replay. It's common for big stars to turn out for teams that aren't their own during the war, but *Evening Telegraph* reporter 'Rambler' states that Matthews' appearance in this match is against the sporting spirit of the knockout competition although he admits that Matthews plays a sterling game. However, young unknown defender Tommy Dunsmore keeps the great Matthews under control. Dunsmore also scores one of United's goals, with Alex Glen and Tommy Adamson getting the others, and although Airdrie get a late consolation goal, United win 3-1 and march on to the final, against Rangers.

SATURDAY 18th APRIL 1925

A draw with Broxburn United at Tannadice is enough to seal the Division Two title for United, with one game left to play. United dominate the first half but much of the finishing is poor and they only score once, through a Bobby Bauld strike from 20 yards. The visitors have very few chances but score twice in the last 15 minutes of the game, with one of their goals coming from a weak shot that rolls through goalie Frank Bridgeford's legs. But Broxburn only have the lead for one minute before William Mackie's equaliser seals the title for United.

SATURDAY 18th APRIL 1942

United beat Rangers 8-1 at Tannadice in the wartime North Eastern League. Rangers score first through a penalty, before United respond through Bobby Gardiner, Jimmy Morgan, debutant Laurie Nevins, David Low, and Albert Juliussen and Bob Glassey, who get two each. 'Rambler', in *The Evening Telegraph*, calls it the best match of the season, and says that Rangers, who had a full-strength team, came up against more than their match.

SATURDAY 19th APRIL 1997

A Lars Zetterlund equaliser against Motherwell in the fourth to last game of the season seals third place in the league and UEFA Cup qualification for United, but Zetterlund has no memory of his goal after the match, after he's knocked unconscious and concussed by a blow to the head.

WEDNESDAY 20th APRIL 1983

For the second time in two weeks, United travel to Glasgow for a league match against Celtic, who are three points ahead of the Terrors. United play a positive attacking game from the start, and get a well-deserved early lead through Paul Hegarty, although Charlie Nicholas equalises with a penalty before half-time. Early in the second half, Eamonn Bannon scores from a penalty, but Richard Gough is sent off with half an hour to go, following a confrontation with Davie Provan. United's ten men start to drop deeper and face waves of Celtic attacks, until Tommy Burns levels the game at 2-2. In spite of the one-man deficit, United, knowing that one point probably won't be enough in the title race, go on the offensive again, whenever they can, and, five minutes from the end, Ralph Milne lobs Pat Bonner, to send the large travelling support wild with joy, and leave the Tangerines just one point off the lead, with four games left to play. Jim McLean describes the performance as magnificent and says that he has never been prouder of his players.

WEDNESDAY 20th APRIL 1988

Dens Park is the venue for the second replay of United's epic Scottish Cup semi-final against Aberdeen. Willie Miller and Alex McLeish are both booked in the first seven minutes for fouls on Kevin Gallacher, who's a constant thorn in the Dons' side, and whose excellent cross sets up Iain Ferguson to score the only goal of the game, 15 minutes from the end, sending the Tangerines into the final.

SATURDAY 20th APRIL 1929

Arbroath draw 0-0 with King's Park while United unexpectedly lose 1-0 at home to Forfar, with the only goal coming when Forfar's David Kilgour charges United goalie Harry McGregor, knocking the ball out of his hands and into the net, shortly after United right-back William Taylor had been carried off injured. It doesn't sound like a great day in United's history, but it's the day when their promotion back into Division One is confirmed, because, with just one game left to play, third-placed Arbroath can no longer catch them. If United can win their last game of the season, they'll go up as champions.

*Paul Hegarty, captain,
top-class defender and
prolific goalscorer*

SATURDAY 21st APRIL 1956

In his first full season at Tannadice after completing his national service, Johnny Coyle gets four goals in one game as the Terrors thrash Berwick Rangers 8-1. Coyle finishes the season on 40 league goals, and 43 goals in all competitions, which is a club record. He scores 38 goals for United in the next season, and 20 the season after that, even though he leaves the club in December 1957.

WEDNESDAY 22nd APRIL 1987

United become the first Scottish club to reach the UEFA Cup Final when they do something that no other side has done in a European game in 17 years: beat Borussia Mönchengladbach away. Borussia – who knocked Rangers out in the third round of the competition – had been dismissive of United's chances, following the goalless draw in the first leg, but in Germany the whole United team come good at the right moment. Both sides carve out good chances, but Billy Thomson makes some impressive saves, and Paul Hegarty and Dave Narey defend as well as Iain Ferguson and Paul Sturrock play in attack. Ferguson gives the Tangerines the lead just before half-time. Late in the second half, Borussia defender Ulrich Borowka hits the post. It's the home side's last chance, and the 1,500 travelling fans are delirious when United seal the victory with the last kick of the game, as Ian Redford takes the ball past goalie Uwe Kamps and smacks it into the net. Jim McLean dances with delight while German fans sportingly applaud the United players. McLean says, 'I always thought we would get to the final, and I'm delighted that it was a magnificent performance that took us there.' He later adds that he rates the achievement higher than winning the Premier Division.

SATURDAY 22nd APRIL 1950

Queen's Park take the lead in the fourth minute of United's last home game of the season, before the Terrors respond by scoring seven. Young Spiders goalie Ronnie Simpson – who will win the European Cup with Celtic 17 years later – makes several good saves, to prevent United getting into double figures. Alec Shaw, Frank Quinn and Andy Dunsmore each get doubles for United, before Peter McKay adds the seventh.

SATURDAY 22nd APRIL 1944

Three thousand fans turn up to see United play a wartime friendly with a Norwegian Forces team, who hold United to a one-goal lead for the first hour, before the Scots score five more and miss a penalty in the last 30 minutes.

SATURDAY 23rd APRIL 1983

With just three league games left to play in the compelling three-way 1982/83 title race, United go top of the table for the first time in the season, as they thrash Kilmarnock 4-0 at Tannadice, with all four goals coming in the first half. But Jim McLean says, 'If they [the players] thought they knew what pressure was about before, they will find out differently now. They have been under pressure all season, but it will be much harder to take now.' He also describes the Terrors' second-half performance as disgraceful.

SATURDAY 24th APRIL 1920

A record crowd for the Forfarshire Cup Final, of 14,000, watch Dundee Hibs beat Dundee 1-0, but the match has to be replayed after the Dundee captain hands the referee a written protest, a couple of minutes before full time, saying that the Hibs striker listed as 'Anderson' is actually Montrose's David Gibb, who's ineligible to play in the game. Dundee Hibs win the replay though, through an early goal from Dan Gibson.

SATURDAY 25th APRIL 1931

One season after being relegated, United seal promotion back up to Division One on the last day of the season, by beating their promotion rivals Dunfermline 2-1, in a winner-takes-all league decider at Tannadice. Denis McCallum opens the scoring for the home side, former rugby player Bobby Lind equalises in the second half when United goalie Bill McCallum blocks his shot but lets it squirm out of his grasp and over the line, and Andy Haddow provides the winning goal for United. *The Courier* reports that 'it would be an exaggeration to say that either side displayed football worthy of the First Division. They did not. Far from it.' But United's George Gardiner does produce a shot so hard that it lays out burly Dunfermline defender Dick Little.

WEDNESDAY 25th APRIL 1984

On a sweltering Italian afternoon, United lose a bad-tempered European Cup semi-final second leg 3-0 to Roma, in front of 68,000 fans in the Stadio Olimpico. Jim McLean later says that it's the only European match when he felt he was in real danger. After the home leg, Italian newspapers printed allegations that United players had taken performance-enhancing drugs, and McLean naively made a joke about it, which was seized on as evidence of guilt, contributing to Roma fans' anger and leading to an intimidating atmosphere in Rome. The atmosphere seems to affect the United players, who play below their capabilities, against very talented opposition. Two goals from Roberto Pruzzo, and an Agostino Di Bartoleome penalty, end United's European Cup dream, and, at the end of the match, Roma players rush across to McLean, Walter Smith and reserve goalie John Gardiner, push and jostle them and shout abuse, while fans pelt the United men with missiles. In his autobiography, McLean says he has never watched his video of the game, because of the misery and heartache the match brought him.

SATURDAY 26th APRIL 2014

Chasing Motherwell for third place in the league and Europa League qualification, United welcome the Steelmen to Tannadice and beat them 5-1. Before kick-off, there's a minute's applause for United legend Frank Kopel, who died recently at the age of 65. And then it's one-way traffic. Stuart Armstrong sets up Nadir Çiftçi to crack home an early opening goal from the edge of the box. Motherwell goalie Gunnar Nielsen makes good saves from Çiftçi and Gary Mackay-Steven, before Çiftçi makes it 2-0 on the stroke of half-time. In the second half, Armstrong hammers the ball into the top corner and Ryan Dow and substitute Brian Graham get goals number four and five.

WEDNESDAY 27th APRIL 1977

Dave Narey becomes the first Dundee United player to play for Scotland when he comes on as a substitute in a friendly against Sweden. Narey goes on to get 35 caps for Scotland, and would surely have got many more if he hadn't played during an era when Scotland had such an embarrassment of central defensive riches, including Willie Miller, Alex McLeish and Alan Hansen.

SUNDAY 27th APRIL 2014

The PFA Scotland Young Player of the Year award goes to Andy Robertson, one of three United players on the shortlist, alongside Stuart Armstrong and Ryan Gauld. Robertson says, 'Stuart and Gauldy have had amazing seasons but I am glad to win it. We have been joking since we were nominated and there were a few laughs. I wouldn't say we were really surprised when the three of us were nominated because we were playing well as a whole team but there has to be credit given to the other players like Paul Paton and John Rankin, who have played well every week and made us tick.'

SATURDAY 27th APRIL 1929

One week after securing promotion, United beat East Stirling 3-1 at Tannadice in the last game of the season, to seal the Division Two championship, but *The Courier* laments that 'the pep and dash which have characterised their play throughout the season were conspicuous by their absence'. But Jimmy Cameron scores twice, either side of half-time, and a Geordie Henderson header gives United a three-goal lead, before the visitors pull one back with the best goal of the game. Irrespective of missing pep and absent dash, United seal a winning end to a successful season.

WEDNESDAY 28th APRIL 1976

Goalie Hamish McAlpine is a goalscoring hero for United as they welcome Hibs to Tannadice for the second to last game of the season. In the first season of the ten-team Premier Division, with two relegation places, the Terrors are in danger of being relegated. Meanwhile, Hibs, who are in third place in the table, are challenging for a place in the UEFA Cup, and with both teams having so much to play for, *The Glasgow Herald* reports that there's a cup-tie atmosphere. In the 12th minute, Hibs' Des Bremner pulls down George Fleming in the box. But United have missed six penalties in the season so far, so McAlpine runs up the pitch and fires the ball home, to score his first ever goal. Six minutes later, Henry Hall gets the only other goal of the game, and the 2-0 win puts United one point above second-bottom Dundee in the relegation battle.

SATURDAY 28th APRIL 1934

The attendance – of 8,700 – for the final league game of the season, against Albion Rovers, is the highest of the season at Tannadice. United need to win the match to avoid finishing second from bottom of Division Two and having to seek re-election, but only about half of the crowd are fans of the home side. Roughly 3,000 are Rovers fans, who've travelled through from Coatbridge on special trains, and it's estimated that about 1,500 Arbroath fans are in the crowd to cheer on United, because, if they win, the Red Lichties – who have played all of their games – will be promoted at Rovers' expense. The match is physical. *The Sunday Post* reports that 'Caution and good football were thrown to the winds. The heat of that 90 minutes of football must have singed the grass!' Writing in *The Courier*, 'The Laird' says 'as the game progressed, the violence of the Rovers' play increased and the fouls were frequent', as the smaller United players 'were falling down like ninepins'. The physicality culminates in a brawl on the touchline, with several fans getting involved. The police have to restore order, while the referee sends off one player from each side. Rovers get three goals in ten minutes in the second half, before Davie Laing scores two penalties for United. The Laird says, 'Rovers left the field Second Division champions, but they did not make many friends at Tannadice.' United are comfortably re-elected at the Scottish League AGM, but the SFA order them to put up signs telling fans not to invade the pitch again.

SATURDAY 29th APRIL 1961

A 5-0 defeat of Dunfermline at Tannadice on the last day of the season, with Dennis Gillespie getting a hat-trick and veteran Neil Mochan scoring twice, ensures that United finish above Dundee in their first season back in the top flight.

TUESDAY 30th APRIL 2002

United goalie Alan Combe plays in goal against United, for Scotland, as Berti Vogts arranges a match for an experimental Scotland side against the Terrors, to give trials to some fringe players. United's Jim Lauchlan comes on as a substitute for the Scotland team, which wins 2-0, through goals from Paul Dalglish and Scott Dobie.

SATURDAY 30th APRIL 1960

The largest crowd of the day in Scotland is at Tannadice in Division Two, as 16,000 fans turn up, in heavy rain, for United's last game of the season – against Berwick Rangers – knowing that victory will earn them promotion back into the top flight for the first time since 1932. Early in the game, centre-forward Tommy Campbell – who Jerry Kerr had bought from Albion Rovers in March – scores his ninth league goal in just seven games. It's the only goal of the game, and the fans know that, depending on results elsewhere, a draw might not be enough. But the Terrors hold onto their lead, and happy fans rush onto the pitch at full time to mob their heroes, especially Campbell and young star defender Ron Yeats.

SATURDAY 30th APRIL 1983

At a cost of £6,000, United pay for 4,100 of their fans to get in to their third-last league game of the season, away to Morton, as they chase the title. The fans create a tremendous atmosphere, at a match that's like a home game for the Terrors. After a nervy first half-hour, an Eamonn Bannon free kick hits the post and Davie Dodds prods it home. After that the Tangerines are on easy street. Dave Narey and Ralph Milne stretch the lead and Dodds gets another, to make it 4-0, while Paul Hegarty plays in goal for most of the second half, as Hamish McAlpine goes off with a thigh injury. Jim McLean says: 'Of course I'm delighted with the win, but even more so by the tremendous response from our supporters.' If United can win their last two league games they'll win the title.

SATURDAY 30th APRIL 1988

Mixu Paatelainen scores all of the goals in a 4-0 defeat of Morton, as Paul Sturrock returns from injury after six months out. William Hunter in *The Glasgow Herald* reports that Sturrock 'played like a kid again, with an excited sense of freedom and uncaged freshness and enthusiasm'. Sturrock sets up Paatelainen's third goal with a characteristic run and cut-back, while the first comes from an Eamonn Bannon cross, the second is a mishit shot that's fumbled by Morton keeper David Wylie, and the big Finn hammers the fourth from distance past Wylie, who barely moves. Unfortunately the Terrors finish the game with ten men, as Paatelainen, Bannon and Iain Ferguson all pick up ankle injuries.

SATURDAY 30th APRIL 1938

United and Airdrie share ten goals in a high-scoring draw at Tannadice. Duncan Hutchison's younger brother, Dan, scores a hat-trick for United, including the equaliser in the final minutes, when a clearance hits his shins and rebounds into the net. The result means that Airdrie miss out on promotion. With the season over, United immediately release all but two of their players, and make the two who are retained – Duncan Hutchison and Don Reid – available for transfer.

DUNDEE UNITED

ON THIS DAY

MAY

TUESDAY 1st MAY 1990

Christian Dailly, Duncan Ferguson and Andy McLaren are among the players who earn United the Scottish Youth Cup. The young Terrors – who lost 1-0 to Celtic in the 1989 final at Tannadice – beat Hibs 4-2 on penalties in the final at Easter Road, after scoring over 20 goals and conceding just one in the whole tournament. Three players – Dailly, Pat Clarke and Eddie Conville – don't have much time to celebrate, as they're back at school sitting exams the next day. Jim McLean says: 'They did very well, and it was particularly encouraging to see them handle the pressure of the penalty shoot-out.' He adds: 'Seven of the team are under-17s, and will be able to play [in the same tournament] again next year.' It's a good point. Twelve months later, United beat Hibs in the final again, 2-0 at Tannadice.

SATURDAY 2nd MAY 1998

In the penultimate game of the season, United beat Hibs 2-1 at Easter Road to save themselves from relegation and send the Edinburgh side down instead. Hibs take the lead through Grant Brebner in the first half, but Kjell Olofsson strikes twice in the last 20 minutes. United manager Tommy McLean laments the league structure that puts relegation pressure on so many clubs, saying: 'It's very sad that a club of Hibs' size should be lost to the elite of Scottish football… It may be exciting, but I don't think a ten-team league is good for the quality of our game. It's had its day and it's time for change.'

MONDAY 2nd MAY 2016

With three games of the season left to play, United lose 2-1 away to Dundee and are relegated, for the first time in 21 years. 'It's simply not good enough, nowhere near good enough,' says Mixu Paatelainen, who had reduced the gap at the bottom of the table after returning to the club as manager seven months earlier. 'They [the players] are honest boys, they try hard, but we need to make so many changes. Not only team-wise but also elsewhere to bounce back stronger.' Unfortunately for the big Finn, he doesn't get a chance to bounce back, as he's sacked the next day.

WEDNESDAY 3rd MAY 1967

Jock Stein's all-conquering Celtic side have to put the champagne on ice as United delay their title celebrations by winning the penultimate game of the season, 3-2 at Parkhead. Twice the Glasgow side have the lead, through Tommy Gemmell and Willie Wallace, but twice United – credited as calm and methodical by *The Glasgow Herald* – equalise, through Billy Hainey and then Dennis Gillespie, before Jackie Graham beats Ronnie Simpson – while United goalie Sandy Davie makes good saves from Wallace and Bobby Lennox – to earn both points for the Terrors, who are the only team to beat Celtic on Scottish soil in their season mirabilis.

SATURDAY 3rd MAY 1958

United beat Berwick Rangers 7-0 in the last game of the season. Jock Keddie, playing as a trialist, scores twice but doesn't play again for United. Dave Sturrock also gets two, while Willie McDonald, Alan Ross and Stewart Fraser score one each.

SATURDAY 4th MAY 1996

On the final day of their first season in the second tier since 1959/60, United head to Greenock for a vital deciding match in the promotion race. United and Morton are level on points, although the Terrors have a vastly superior goal difference, as they compete for the play-off spot – or possibly top place and promotion, if leaders Dunfermline lose or draw against Airdrie at the same time. A capacity crowd packs into Cappielow for a match that's notable more for drama than quality. United take the lead early on through a Brian Welsh header from a corner, but the home side equalise early in the second half when Craig Brewster somehow heads a Morton corner into his own net to score an own goal that would have been very impressive if it had come at the other end. Just two minutes later the Tangerines retake the lead with the simplest of goals, as Brewster flicks Steven Pressley's long ball to Robbie Winters, who heads it into the net. And then Airdrie equalise at East End Park, which briefly puts United top, but Morton and Dunfermline each score within a couple of minutes of each other, and the Tangerines end up in the play-offs, where they will face Partick Thistle.

TUESDAY 4th MAY 1976

Early in Jim McLean's time at Tannadice, with the top flight cut back to ten teams for the first time, and with two relegation places, it takes a last-day-of-the-season 0-0 draw with Rangers, who've just won the treble, to save United from relegation, on goal difference. The home side and their fans are more interested in celebrating their achievements than they are in the league fixture, parading their trophies on the pitch and having a game between two Rangers veterans' teams before the United match kicks off. But in spite of Rangers' welcome ambivalence, Hamish McAlpine still has to make three good saves in the second half to preserve the Terrors' top-flight status. Six minutes before full time, George Fleming is brought down in the box and United win a penalty, which McAlpine – fresh from recent spot-kick success against Hibs – runs up the pitch to take, to earn instant safety, but he cracks it against the post and then must sprint back to his own goal. There are no more scares though, and United stay up, while Dundee go down instead. There are so many glories in United's history that probably wouldn't have happened if Rangers had scored just once on this day.

SATURDAY 4th MAY 1929

With the help of a bit of luck, United win their third trophy in one season. The men from Tannadice – who've already won the Second Division and the Forfarshire Cup – draw the Fleming Shield Final 2-2 with Aberdeen at Pittodrie, with United's goals coming from Jacky Kay and Jimmy Cameron. The clubs agree to settle the tie by tossing a coin, and United are the lucky winners.

SATURDAY 4th MAY 2019

Striker Chris Mochrie becomes United's youngest ever player when he comes on as a substitute in a 1-0 defeat away to Morton. After the match, he says: 'It was an unbelievable feeling to make my debut. I was excited when I was told I would be in the squad and to have got on the park was amazing.' Shortly after the game, Mochrie signs full-time for United, although he still plans to return to school after the summer to do his Highers.

SATURDAY 4th MAY 1974

United play in their first ever Scottish Cup Final, against Celtic in front of 76,000 fans at Hampden. One Celtic fan, Billy Connolly, says he has divided loyalties because of his relationship with Dundee Folk Club. Unfortunately, not everyone is so magnanimous, as fighting breaks out on the terraces, 125 people are arrested and 40 are taken to hospital, and there's also relatively innocent disobedience when two dogs wander onto the pitch and stop play. On the pitch, it's not United's day, as Celtic score two quick goals in the first half. Andy Gray and Archie Knox both come close to pulling one back but the only other goal comes from Celtic's Dixie Deans, in the last minute. United do, however, qualify for the European Cup Winners' Cup, because Celtic have also won the league. One United player who won't be competing in that tournament is goalie Sandy Davie. The cup final is his 184th and last appearance before he emigrates to New Zealand, where he ends up playing for their national team.

SATURDAY 4th MAY 1940

Despite transport restrictions and petrol rationing, dozens of coaches and several special trains take United fans to Hampden for the War Cup Final, against Rangers. In front of an estimated crowd of 90,000 – and with thousands more locked outside – United's Tommy Adamson has the ball in the net in the first half, but – as the dejected Rangers players head back up the pitch for kick-off – it's harshly ruled out for offside, before Jimmy Smith gets the only goal of the game, for the Ibrox side, 15 minutes from the end. And in the last minute, Light Blues defender Dougie Gray blocks a Jimmy Robertson lob, to bring an end to United's cup hopes.

SATURDAY 5th MAY 1990

Free transport to Paisley is laid on for United fans for the last game of a transitional season, away to St Mirren, with the Tangerines needing a draw to finish in fourth place. Not much happens – except for the Buddies hitting the post twice within a couple of seconds – in the match, which finishes goalless, and fourth place is enough to get United into the UEFA Cup, after Aberdeen win the Scottish Cup.

WEDNESDAY 6th MAY 1987

Four thousand travelling United fans are among the 50,000 crowd as the Terrors step onto the biggest stage in the club's history, in the first leg of the UEFA Cup Final, against a strong IFK Gothenburg side – who'd narrowly lost the European Cup semi-final to Barcelona on penalties the year before – in their Ullevi Stadium. Unfortunately, the pitch is in terrible condition, and United can't play their usual passing game. Their prospects aren't helped when goalie Billy Thomson takes a head knock in the first half, which needs five stitches, and a Kjell Petterson downward header in 38 minutes bounces over him and into the net. United can't get a valuable away goal, and the match finishes 1-0 to the home side, but still the final is finely poised, with Gothenburg coach Gunder Bengtsson predicting that the Tannadice leg will be the Swedes' hardest game of the tournament.

SATURDAY 7th MAY 1983

With the league title in touching distance, United seem nervous early on against Motherwell at a noisy Tannadice, in the penultimate game of the season. But the nerves are shaken off after 25 minutes when Eamonn Bannon opens the scoring with a brilliant free kick. Bannon gets another and Davie Dodds also scores twice as United take another big step towards their first ever league title. Now the Tangerines just have to win at Dens Park on the last day of the season to seal the championship.

SATURDAY 8th MAY 1982

As they battle with St Mirren for UEFA Cup qualification, United beat league leaders Celtic 3-0 at home in the penultimate game of the season, denting the Glaswegians' title hopes. Paul Hegarty opens the scoring with a first-half header, Paul Sturrock doubles the lead just 20 seconds into the second half, from a Hamish McAlpine long ball, and, ten minutes from the end, Ralph Milne swerves past Roy Aitken and cracks the ball past Pat Bonner, sealing an emphatic victory with an appropriately impressive strike. Celtic manager Billy McNeill says, 'They [United] played as I hoped we would play', and *The Glasgow Herald*'s Jim Reynolds reports that 'United looked the side with the quality of champions'. Well, maybe next season.

SATURDAY 9th MAY 1981

United play in their second ever Scottish Cup final, against Rangers. The Terrors spurn several chances, and Rangers goalie Jim Stewart spectacularly saves a curling Eamonn Bannon free kick. The match culminates, dramatically, in a last-minute penalty for the Light Blues. Future United player Ian Redford – who had scored from the spot against the Tangerines a month earlier – takes it but his shot hits diving Hamish McAlpine's legs and rebounds to safety, as the referee blows for full time. The replay is scheduled for the following Tuesday.

FRIDAY 10th MAY 1974

Dave Narey, at the age of 17, scores his first goal for United, in a 4-2 defeat of Morton, while midfielder Duncan MacLeod gets a hat-trick – three-quarters of all of the goals that he will ever score for United.

FRIDAY 11th MAY 2018

United go into the Premiership play-off semi-final second leg away to Livingston trailing 3-2 after losing at home. The West Lothian side take an early lead, before Scott Fraser beats two defenders and equalises with a low shot. Scott McDonald and Billy King play particularly well for the Tangerines, but Livi goalie Neil Alexander makes a series of good saves, and the Terrors are consigned to another season in the Championship.

TUESDAY 12th MAY 1981

After playing so well in the Scottish Cup Final, United face a much-improved Rangers in the replay. Davie Cooper scores one and sets up two as the Light Blues win 4-1. Davie Dodds scores United's goal, after Paul Sturrock knocks an Eamonn Bannon cross to him, but the result is a terrible anti-climax at the end of a long season.

SATURDAY 13th MAY 1989

Fans are allowed into Tannadice for free for the last game of the season, against Hamilton, but *The Glasgow Herald* reports that most of them would have paid to be let out before the end, as United lose to their bottom-of-the-table opponents. The game is Paul Sturrock's 575th and last for United.

WEDNESDAY 13th MAY 1970

In Mexico City, ahead of the World Cup, United play a friendly against a team who are originally billed as club side Leon, but who turn out to be almost entirely players from Mexico's World Cup squad, and not from Leon. Unfortunately, playing at altitude, United lose 6-0, even though they frequently catch the Mexicans in their offside trap. *The Evening Telegraph* reports that Mexico's keeper, Ignacio Calderón, only has to touch the ball four times.

SATURDAY 13th MAY 1995

United lose 1-0 at home to Celtic on the last day of the season and are relegated, one year after winning the Scottish Cup. With players like Maurice Malpas, Gordan Petrić, Jim McInally, Billy McKinlay, Christian Dailly and Craig Brewster in the team, United seem too good to go down, but earning just four points from their last 11 league games consigns them to the drop.

SATURDAY 14th MAY 1983

The excitement, anticipation and nerves are unmistakable as almost 30,000 fans pack in to Dens Park on the greatest day in United's history. In the Dundee derby – the last match of a relentlessly captivating league title race – United know that nothing less than a win can guarantee them their first ever league title. It all starts so well when Ralph Milne scores with a spectacular 25-yard lob in the fourth minute, and Eamonn Bannon doubles the lead seven minutes later, knocking home the rebound after keeper Colin Kelly saves his penalty. But the script shifts disconcertingly when Iain Ferguson pulls one back for the Dark Blues, and, with just one goal in it, the fans face a nervous hour-long wait for the final whistle, which brings glorious relief as it confirms the dream-like news that United have finished the season one point ahead of Celtic and Aberdeen, with a joint record points total and a joint record total goals scored for the Premier League. As someone is sent to buy some champagne, the celebrating players lift a smiling Jim McLean onto their shoulders – at the end of a season when a core of just 12 players played ten or more league games – and thousands of fans join in the open-top bus celebration in City Square the next day.

*Jim McLean, the mastermind
of United's remarkable league
championship victory*

SATURDAY 14th MAY 1988

Both sets of fans show Prime Minister Margaret Thatcher red cards, in protest at her NHS policies, as she visits Hampden for the Scottish Cup Final, between United and Celtic. On the pitch, early in the second half, Kevin Gallacher outruns Roy Aitken and fires the ball past Allen McKnight, but two late Frank McAvennie goals turn the game on its head, as, for the fifth time, United leave a Scottish Cup Final with silver medals. SFA secretary Ernie Walker, relieved that the protests against the Prime Minister hadn't been nastier, says, 'Dundee United's supporters showed why they were given FIFA's Fair Play Award.'

SATURDAY 15th MAY 2010

United win the Scottish Cup for the second time ever. The Terrors dominate against Ross County, but the match remains goalless until the 60th minute, when David Goodwillie's stunning lob from the edge of the box breaks the deadlock. Fifteen minutes later, Craig Conway collects the ball from a Goodwillie flick, bursts forward and beats Staggies keeper Michael McGovern. And five minutes later Morgaro Gomis flicks the ball to Conway, who scores his second and the Terrors' third, to cap a great day for 28,000 happy Arabs in the Hampden sunshine. United boss Peter Houston says 'We're absolutely delighted. I'm so happy. I think there's going to be a massive party in Dundee.' There is. The next day there's a parade in the City Square, followed by more celebrations at Tannadice.

SATURDAY 16th MAY 1987

The Scottish Cup Final is sandwiched between the two legs of the UEFA Cup Final, and United start it as clear favourites, against St Mirren. But, so close to the end of such a long season, a poor match doesn't go well for the Terrors. After 90 goalless minutes, an Iain Ferguson goal is ruled out for offside in extra time when Kevin Gallacher is deemed to be interfering with play, and then the Buddies' Ian Ferguson scores the only goal of the game, leaving Jim McLean – who dismissed talk of a Hampden hoodoo before this final but admits afterwards that he's not so sure – lamenting the fact that too many United players 'fell well below the standards they have set for themselves'.

THURSDAY 16th MAY 1996

After drawing the away leg of the Premiership play-off final against Partick Thistle 1-1, United win a dramatic second leg at a packed Tannadice. There are no goals for the first 70 minutes, but then the Jags go in front through a soft penalty. The Tangerines throw everything at Partick, but it looks like they'll have to play another season in the second flight and excited anticipation is building among the away fans, until, in the last minute of normal time, Andy McLaren sends in a cross, Owen Coyle nods it back across the goal and Brian Welsh heads home. And five minutes from the end of extra time, Coyle turns home the winner, to send the Terrors straight back up to the Premier League, as celebrating fans pour onto the pitch at full time.

SATURDAY 17th MAY 2003

A large group of Arabs travel through to Glasgow to see United take on Partick in the penultimate league game of the season, as they fight to avoid relegation. Jim Paterson scores the only goal of the game, which makes United safe. At full time, Derek Lilley, playing his 90th and last game for the Tangerines, throws his shirt into the crowd, who've been chanting his name. He says: 'The fans have been brilliant, and I'm delighted that they will [still] be watching Premier League football. It was emotional when they sang my name and at the end I wanted to show them how much they mean to me. I hope whoever caught my shirt, it means as much to them as wearing it did to me.'

FRIDAY 17th MAY 2019

United ease into the Premiership play-off final as they beat Inverness Caley Thistle 3-0 at Tannadice, and 4-0 on aggregate. Goalie Ben Siegrest makes some good saves in the first half, before Nicky Clark opens the scoring from the penalty spot in stoppage time at the end of the first half. Osman Sow gets his first goal for United, taking the ball with his back to goal before turning and firing home, before Clark hits both posts, and substitute Sam Stanton sets up his fellow sub Pavol Šafranko to make it three, setting up a final against St Mirren.

SATURDAY 17th MAY 2014

On a disappointing day at Celtic Park, a strong United team, including Andy Robertson, Ryan Gauld, Stuart Armstrong, Gary Mackay-Steven and Nadir Çiftçi, twice hit the post as they lose the Scottish Cup Final 2-0 against St Johnstone. Manager Jackie McNamara says: 'It just wasn't our day, little thin margins like the post and the bar. I think we can play a lot better. We had chances but there's a thin line between winning and losing sometimes.' The final is Robertson and Gauld's last game in tangerine, as they leave for Hull and Sporting Lisbon.

SATURDAY 18th MAY 1991

United lose one of the most dramatic Scottish Cup finals ever, 4-3 against a strong Motherwell side, who are managed by Jim McLean's brother Tommy and who have Tom Boyd, Phil O'Donnell and Davie Cooper in their team. In the first seven minutes, the Terrors – playing in white – have a goal ruled out for offside and hit a post, but it's the Steelmen who open the scoring, through Iain Ferguson, and although Dave Bowman equalises, Motherwell score twice more to lead 3-1 after 65 minutes. But United hit back, through John O'Neil – the fourth goal in a 12-minute period – and a brave Darren Jackson header in the last minute, which sends the United fans wild. The momentum is with the Tangerines, but it's Motherwell who get the winner in extra time, and their goalie Ally Maxwell saves well from Maurice Malpas near the end as, once again, United are denied glory at Hampden. Malpas refutes suggestions of a 'Hampden hoodoo', saying 'on each occasion, we have failed to do ourselves justice and have left empty-handed. It's as simple as that.'

FRIDAY 18th MAY 1923

At the Annual General Meeting of the Scottish League, Dundee Hibs – who, after being relegated from Division Two in 1922, have spent a disappointing season playing in a league called the Scottish Alliance, which is mostly made up of clubs' reserve teams – are voted back into Division Two, replacing East Stirling, who are relegated to the new Division Three. Dundee Hibs had been offered a place in Division Three, but worked hard to convince clubs to let them back into Division Two instead.

SATURDAY 19th MAY 1979

Paul Hegarty becomes the second United player to play for Scotland. Alan Hansen, George Burley and John Wark also make their international debuts in the same game, as part of a young, experimental side who unfortunately lose to Wales.

SATURDAY 19th MAY 1951

B Division Dundee United beat Dundee – who've just finished third in the A Division – 3-2 in the Forfarshire Cup Final in front of 12,000 fans, less than 24 hours after beating Brechin 6-1 in the semi-final. Peter McKay scores twice and George Cruickshank gets one, before the Terrors fill the cup with champagne and are toasted by city MP Tom Cook.

WEDNESDAY 20th MAY 1987

Four days after playing 120 minutes in the Scottish Cup Final, United must pick themselves up again for their 67th game of the season: the UEFA Cup Final second leg, in front of 21,000 fans at a packed Tannadice, on a night when Jim McLean can't bring himself to look at the trophy, in case it brings bad luck. The Tangerines, back on their own turf, can play their usual passing game, and have some early chances, but Lennart Nilsson gives Gothenburg the lead after 20 minutes, leaving United needing three goals. McLean shuffles his pack at half-time and pushes John Clark forward, and it's Clark who gets the equaliser, with a powerful shot from the edge of the area. For the last half-hour United push almost everyone forward but the Swedes defend well and earn the trophy for the second time in five years. Both teams do a lap of honour, applauding all of the fans, who all applaud them back. United fans throw their scarves to Gothenburg players, who pick them up and wave. Almost an hour after full time, the home fans are still there, applauding Jim McLean. McLean says, 'The players gave every solitary ounce they had. We just had nothing left when we needed it most. Gothenburg are a fine side.' He adds: 'This has been the hardest season I've ever had here in every way.' Gothenburg coach Gunder Bengtsson says, 'There was little between the teams.' The United fans' generous spirit is rewarded with the first ever FIFA Fair Play Award.

SUNDAY 21st MAY 2000

Nineteen years after his debut, Maurice Malpas makes his 830th and last appearance for United, at the age of 38, in a last-day-of-the-season 2-0 defeat to Celtic. Malpas – a key player in the United teams who won the league and reached the European Cup semi-final and the UEFA Cup Final, and the captain of the Scottish Cup-winning team – remains at Tannadice as a coach.

SATURDAY 21st MAY 2005

United go into the last game of the season, away against Inverness Caley Thistle, knowing that a draw or a win will save them from relegation. The Terrors are on top for most of the first half but Caley Thistle goalie Mark Brown makes some good saves. The breakthrough finally comes in the 82nd minute, when Barry Robson is fouled in the penalty box and blasts the spot kick home. He runs to celebrate with the travelling fans behind the goal, sparking wild celebrations and a pitch invasion. Caley Thistle manager Craig Brewster – a man with United in his heart, of course – pleads with referee Alan Freeland not to book Robson, who's already had one yellow card. The whistler relents, but a few minutes later, he does send Robson off, giving him a second yellow card for a dive. But United are safe, and it's Dundee who are relegated.

WEDNESDAY 21st MAY 1969

Dundee United – playing in the NASL International Cup five-team league tournament, in the USA, under the guise of Dallas Tornado – lose 3-1 to West Ham, who are known as Baltimore Bays during the tournament. In tiring Texas humidity, Kenny Cameron opens the scoring for the Tornado, and misses a penalty, but Martin Peters sets up Geoff Hurst to equalise, before Trevor Brooking gives the visitors the lead, from a Harry Redknapp pass, and Peters makes it 3-1 with a spectacular header. Bobby Moore is also among the all-star Bays team. Under the tournament's innovative points system, the Tornado get one league point for the goal they score in the game, while the Bays get nine: six for the win, and one for each goal. Six games into the tournament, the Tornado are on 15 points, while the Bays are on 35, behind Wolves, who are on 46.

SATURDAY 21st MAY 1994

It's seventh Scottish Cup Final lucky for United, as they beat Rangers to lift the famous old trophy for the first time. Manager Ivan Golac encourages the players to relax before the game, letting them go to the horse racing at Hamilton, and it seems to do the trick. The Tangerines have a strong penalty appeal turned down in the tenth minute, when Alec Cleland is fouled. But it doesn't matter, because, at the start of the second half, Christian Dailly nicks the ball from Rangers goalie Ally Maxwell, his shot hits the post and Craig Brewster runs in to score his 20th goal of the season. United hold out comfortably for the rest of the match, sparking wild celebrations as they finally claim the trophy that has eluded them for so long. Back in Dundee in the evening, Jim McInally and Dave Bowman take the cup out to the Smugglers pub, and thousands of fans turn out the next day to celebrate with their cup-winning heroes.

SUNDAY 22nd MAY 1988

Tony Andreu is born on this day in Cagnes-Sur-Mer in France. He joins United on a year-long loan in 2016 and is top scorer at Tannadice in 2016/17, as the Tangerines narrowly miss out on promotion.

FRIDAY 23rd MAY 1969

In their sixth game in the 1969 NASL International Cup, United, playing as Dallas Tornado, get their first win, beating Kilmarnock, who are playing as St Louis – and who have Jim McLean in their side – 1-0 away. The only goal of the game comes at the start of the second half, when Ian Mitchell sets up Davie Wilson, who goes past two defenders and beats Sandy McLaughlin in goal. That's seven points to the Tornado, who leapfrog St Louis at the bottom of the table.

SUNDAY 24th MAY 2015

On the last day of the season, Nadir Çiftçi scores twice in his last game for United, a 3-0 derby win at Dens Park, with the other goal coming from Blair Spittal, as the Terrors finish the season in fifth place in the Premiership.

MONDAY 24th MAY 1909

Dundee Hibs are formed, at a meeting at the Crown Hotel. With some First Division players pledging to play for the new club – who are due to take over the tenancy of Tannadice four days later – a letter requesting entry into the Second Division is written, to be sent to every club in the league.

TUESDAY 25th MAY 1982

United defender Gary McGinnis scores a late equaliser for Scotland against the Netherlands at the European Under-18 Championships, to send Scotland through to the second round of the tournament, which they go on to win. Marco van Basten had opened the scoring. McGinnis goes on to play 92 times for United.

WEDNESDAY 26th MAY 1965

On a Tannadice pitch that's been turned into a mudbath by heavy rain, United beat Partick 3-0 in the Summer Cup semi-final second leg, after drawing the away leg 0-0. Ian Mitchell taps in the opening goal after 28 minutes when Thistle defender Jackie Campbell slips as he's trying to deal with a Finn Døssing cross. But the match remains open until the 75th minute, when Døssing cracks a shot in off the underside of the crossbar, before Mitchell adds his second and United's third. The Summer Cup, which was originally a wartime tournament, was brought back in 1964 but only lasts for two seasons.

SUNDAY 26th MAY 2019

United take St Mirren to penalties in the Premiership play-off final second leg, but then it all goes painfully wrong as Buddies goalie Václav Hladký saves three of the Tangerines' first four spot kicks and the other hits the post. The silver lining for United is that the Dundee derby returns for the new season, following the Dark Blues' relegation. United boss Robbie Neilson says, 'We're moving in the right direction and Dundee United will be back, it just won't be this year.'

THURSDAY 27th MAY 1909

Fledgling Dundee Hibs receive confirmation from the SFA that their application for membership has been accepted.

SUNDAY 28th MAY 2017

United visit Hamilton for the second leg of the Premiership play-off final, after drawing the home leg 0-0. Greg Docherty scores for the home side after 64 minutes and unfortunately United can't find an equaliser, with Simon Murray firing just over the bar and having a shot saved in the dying minutes.

TUESDAY 29th MAY 1923

Dundee Hibs appoint former Scotland goalkeeper Jimmy Brownlie as player-manager. *The Courier* says 'the management of the team could not be in better hands'. They're soon proved right.

MONDAY 29th MAY 1967

At the Cotton Bowl Stadium in Dallas, United, playing in tangerine and blue, under the name Dallas Tornado, win their opening match in the United Soccer Association: a precursor to the NASL, where 12 clubs from around the world are franchised to play under American names. Finn Døssing scores the only goal of the game, against Chicago Mustangs, who are represented by Cagliari.

TUESDAY 29th MAY 1979

Ray Stewart scores a hat-trick in Hiroshima as United beat Burma's national side 4-0 in the Japan Cup, a tournament that also features Tottenham and Fiorentina, among other sides.

THURSDAY 30th MAY 1991

Dundee chairman Angus Cook defends his plans to merge Dundee and Dundee United, and reveals that he has registered the name Dundee City for an amalgamated club, which he thinks could be operating by 1992. Mr Cook, who is offering to buy shares in United to facilitate his plan, cites 'commercial reality' as a barrier to simply investing in his own club instead. Dundee United Supporters' Association spokesman Finlay McKay says: 'When we first heard about it we treated it as a bit of a laugh. But, after reading the reports in the paper today, I know a lot of Dundee United fans will be worried.' He adds: 'Mr Cook's club are languishing in the First Division and are deep in debt. Dundee United are consistently in the top flight of the Premier League and have money in the bank.'

MONDAY 31st MAY 1909

At their annual meeting, the Scottish League teams vote on whether to accept applications for league membership from Dundee Hibs, Renton (who had had to retire from the league 11 years earlier), Johnstone and Wishaw Thistle. But the clubs vote overwhelmingly to retain Arthurlie and Cowdenbeath – who completed the season in the bottom two league places – instead. Dundee Hibs apply to play in the Northern League instead.

SATURDAY 31st MAY 1969

In the last of their eight games at the NASL International Cup, United/ Dallas Tornado beat top-of-the-league Wolves/Kansas City Spurs 3-2 at the Cotton Bowl, earning nine points, to finish third in the tournament. *The Glasgow Herald* calls United's performance sparkling, as Ian Mitchell scores twice and Ian Scott gets one.

DUNDEE UNITED

ON THIS DAY

JUNE

MONDAY 1st JUNE 1931

Following boss Jimmy Brownlie's surprise departure, United appoint his replacement: Albion Rovers manager Willie Reid, a former Rangers and Scotland centre-forward. Reid arrives at Tannadice with a reputation for talent-spotting, but financial problems hamper his stewardship and he leaves three years later.

MONDAY 2nd JUNE 1913

When Division One is expanded from 18 to 20 teams, ambitious Dundee Hibs, despite finishing the season 10th in 14-team Division Two, apply for promotion, and only narrowly miss out when they come third out of seven candidates in the voting, behind Ayr United and Dumbarton.

SATURDAY 2nd JUNE 1979

United line up against Fiorentina in the Japan Cup semi-final without Paul Hegarty and David Narey, who are on international duty, or Hamish McAlpine, who has returned to Scotland after a disagreement with Jim McLean. Twenty-two-year-old goalkeeper Andy Graham stands in for McAlpine and seizes his chance to shine, saving three penalties: the first late in the match, with the score tied at 1-1, and the other two in the penalty shoot-out, to send the Tangerines into the final, against Spurs.

WEDNESDAY 2nd JUNE 1965

Many games in the Summer Cup suffered from low attendances since its reintroduction in 1964, but over 18,000 fans turn out at Tannadice for the second leg of the 1965 final, as the Terrors try to overturn Motherwell's 3-1 lead from a first leg that *The Glasgow Herald* described as exhilarating. Finn Døssing scores after 14 minutes and the *Herald* reports that United have five attacks to each of Motherwell's, but the Steelmen's 'efficient and adaptable' defence holds firm, and United are denied on aggregate.

WEDNESDAY 3rd JUNE 1992

Maurice Malpas captains Scotland, in a friendly against Norway in Oslo, as he becomes the 17th player to reach 50 caps for the national team. The match – a disappointing 0-0 draw – is the last game before Scotland appear at Euro 92, with United players Jim McInally, Dave Bowman, Duncan Ferguson and Malpas in their squad.

MONDAY 4th JUNE 1979

At Tokyo's Olympic Stadium, United, who are already without Paul Hegarty, Dave Narey and Hamish McAlpine, line up for the Japan Cup Final against Tottenham without Davie Dodds, who was taken ill at a reception held by a whisky company, or Ray Stewart, who has joined up with the Scotland under-21 side for a match against Norway. Andy Graham deputises in goal for McAlpine again, in spite of suffering from glandular problems. United win a first-half penalty when Paul Sturrock is brought down, but Walter Smith's spot kick is saved, and Gordon Smith and Ossie Ardiles both score in the second half to win the tournament for Spurs. Jim McLean is full of praise for his team, saying: 'None of my players was outshone by the great Ardiles, and that speaks volumes for our performances. In the past I have tended to undersell the abilities of my players, but not any more. They have proved a lot both to themselves and to me throughout the tournament. After their performances over here against top teams, I can hardly wait for the start of our season back home.'

TUESDAY 5th JUNE 1973

Andy McLaren is born on this day, in Glasgow. He comes through the Dundee United youth system and earns three Scotland under-21 caps, and becomes a Tannadice regular, playing as a winger, when Ivan Golac arrives in Dundee. He's central to the Tangerines' Scottish Cup-winning side, and plays a key part in promotion two years later, before leaving in 1999, before briefly returning to Tannadice in 2003. A favourite with the fans, McLaren plays 250 times for the Tangerines.

MONDAY 6th JUNE 1966

United get their biggest win of a summer tour of Iceland and Denmark, beating an Icelandic FA team 6-0. Shortly after the match, the team fly to Denmark, touching down briefly at Glasgow Airport, where the players get a chance to quickly phone their friends and families before getting onto the Denmark plane. *The Evening Telegraph* reports that 'Keeper Donald Mackay was luckier than most – his wife travelled down from Perth for a quick hello and goodbye!' United win all five games of the tour, scoring 26 goals.

TUESDAY 7th JUNE 1910

With Ayr Parkhouse and Ayr FC combining to form Ayr United, an extra vacancy opens up in the Second Division. Pat Reilly has been intensely canvassing the league clubs, telling them about extensive ground improvements at Tannadice and speculating about the untapped potential of Dundee's 50,000 Irish population, so it's perhaps unsurprising that Dundee Hibs – even though they're just a year old – are elected into the league, with twice as many votes as St Johnstone.

SATURDAY 7th JUNE 1969

Dennis Gillespie gets the only goal of the game as United beat Juventus 1-0 in a friendly in New Jersey, but the result is overshadowed by controversy and anger. Play is held up for five minutes following an argument about substitutions, and as United play their passing game, the Juve players start to hack them down, and *The Evening Telegraph* reports that trainer Andy Dickson is seldom off the field as he attends to injuries. And then, when Andy Rolland is brought down, the American referee sends him off, along with his opponent, although Rolland has done nothing wrong. Mounted police are deployed on the track as anger builds in the crowd of 4,000, who throw cans towards the pitch at the end of the match, while Jerry Kerr brands the refereeing ridiculous.

SUNDAY 8th JUNE 1986

Scotland line up against West Germany at the World Cup in Mexico with four Dundee United players – Richard Gough, Dave Narey, Maurice Malpas and Eamonn Bannon – in their side. As the Scots play well but lose 2-1 to the eventual finalists, Bannon has two good shots well saved by Harald Schumacher, while Gough – who's involved in the build-up for Gordon Strachan's opening goal, and whose header goes narrowly over the bar late on – is attracting interest from English clubs.

TUESDAY 9th JUNE 1925

George Cruickshank is born on this day. He goes on to become a junior Scotland internationalist and to sign, as a left-winger, for United, where he makes 186 appearances and scores 32 goals, in a celebrated forward line alongside Frank Quinn, George Grant, Peter McKay and Andy Dunsmore.

MONDAY 10th JUNE 2013

Twenty-three-year-old striker Johnny Russell completes a £750,000 transfer from United to Derby County. The Tangerines contact Blackburn Rovers about bringing David Goodwillie back to Tannadice as a replacement for Russell, but the Lancashire side reject United's offer.

SATURDAY 10th JUNE 1972

At the end of a gruelling five-match tour of Nigeria, played in such heat that many players plead to be substituted, Hamish McAlpine has to play in an outfield position, with the United team down to the bare bones. The players lose an average of roughly half a stone each in this day's match, a 4-1 defeat to Stationery Stores – one of the most successful clubs in Nigeria at the time – which is played in temperatures in the mid-thirties. Because of the effect of the tour, Jim McLean gives the players an extra week off to recuperate before pre-season training. United win one, draw two and lose two of the matches on the tour. Years later, it's claimed that, because of United's perceived poor performances, 'Dundee United' becomes derogatory slang in parts of Nigeria, but another, at least as plausible, theory hypothesises that the slang term is spread by cheeky Dundee fans when Nigeria come to Scotland for the 1989 under-16 World Cup.

WEDNESDAY 11th JUNE 1919

Dundee Hibs withdraw from the Scottish League in protest about the decision not to reintroduce second division football following the end of World War I. Instead, they play for one season in a new Eastern League, which they win.

SATURDAY 12th JUNE 1909

The Northern League – who have lost six member clubs to the new Central League – vote, at their annual meeting at the Crown Hotel, to accept Dundee Hibs' application. The club will spend its first season playing league matches against Brechin, Montrose, Forfar, Dundee Wanderers, and Dundee and Aberdeen's B teams.

SATURDAY 13th JUNE 1992

Dave Narey wins an MBE for services to football in Scotland, in the Queen's birthday honours list.

WEDNESDAY 14th JUNE 1967

In their fifth game playing as Dallas Tornado in the United Soccer Association, United draw 2-2 in Texas with Toronto City, who are usually much better known as Hibs. The enthusiastic crowd are treated to three goals in the last ten minutes of the first half, with Dennis Gillespie giving the Tornado the lead, before Peter Cormack and Colin Stein both score for the visitors. Billy Hainey secures a point for the Tornado when he blasts home a second-half free kick from 25 yards.

TUESDAY 15th JUNE 1982

Dave Narey becomes the first United player to play for Scotland at the World Cup, as he comes on as a substitute in the 5-2 defeat of New Zealand in Málaga. Meanwhile, Jim McLean is in the dug-out, as Alex Ferguson's assistant manager.

SATURDAY 16th JUNE 1990

United's Maurice Malpas is part of the Scotland side that earn their fourth ever win at a World Cup, as they beat Sweden 2-1 in Genoa.

SATURDAY 17th JUNE 1989

In front of 10,000 fans at Pittodrie, United's John Lindsay – who also scored against Cuba in the group stage – scores the only goal of the game, late on, as Scotland beat highly rated East Germany 1-0, to qualify for the semi-finals of the under-16 World Cup. Lindsay also sets up the only goal in the semi-final against Portugal at a packed Tynecastle three days later, with Brian O'Neil heading home from his corner. Lindsay's career is, unfortunately, cut short by a knee injury.

FRIDAY 18th JUNE 1982

In the heat of Seville, United's Dave Narey scores his first goal for Scotland, against Brazil at the World Cup, opening the scoring with a powerful shot from the edge of the area, and then celebrating as if he can't believe what he's just done. But Zico equalises with an excellent free kick, and, in the second half, with Socrates pulling the strings, Brazil turn on the style and add three more without reply.

Dave Narey, apparently effortless but relentlessly effective, for United and Scotland

WEDNESDAY 19th JUNE 1963

In what is now Malawi, in the first match of a four-week tour of southern Africa, United beat a Nyasaland Select team 10-2 in the city of Blantyre, with four goals from Ian Mitchell, two each from Benny Rooney and Dennis Gillespie, and one apiece for Jim Irvine and Wattie Carlyle. After the match, United head to Harare, 300 miles away, before their next game, on the Sunday, 400 miles further on from Harare, in Zambia.

TUESDAY 20th JUNE 1989

At the age of 32, Paul Sturrock retires as a player and moves full-time into coaching at Tannadice. Meanwhile, the club end speculation about Jim McLean being replaced as manager. Vice-chairman Dr Harry Leadbitter says: 'We've looked long and hard at possible replacements for the manager. Unfortunately, we have failed to find someone of the calibre of Jim McLean so he will remain in charge of the team.' For the first time since Walter Smith moved to Ibrox in 1986 however, McLean – who's keen to concentrate on his role as chairman – does get an assistant manager, as former Dundee and Aberdeen midfielder Steve Murray is appointed.

WEDNESDAY 21st JUNE 1967

United finally click as Dallas Tornado, when they beat Boston Rovers – who are represented by Shamrock Rovers – 4-1, away, with three of the Tornado's goals coming in the first half. United goalie Sandy Davie says: 'The pitch at Boston was one of the worst I've ever seen. It was bumpy and full of holes. Some were filled with soil. The dressing rooms, too, were dreadful. So filthy, [trainer] Andy Dickson had to clean all the seats before we could use them. During the second half we had our first taste of supporters running wild. The referee gave us a throw-in which could have gone either way. Tommy Neilson wandered over to take the throw – and somebody let fly at him with a tomato. The ref stopped the game and called a policeman to watch the part of the crowd from which came the missile.' It's not all bad, though. Davie also says that the players are stocking up on cheap transistor radios and tape recorders. He says, 'I hope the Customs are kind to us when we get home.'

FRIDAY 22nd JUNE 1979

Peter Bonetti, the 37-year-old former England goalkeeper, signs for United. The move comes after Hamish McAlpine was suspended following a disagreement with Jim McLean in Japan, but McLean denies that the two events are related or that McAlpine will be transferred. Bonetti's signing is, however, a clear exception to McLean's rule that all of his players must live in Dundee, as Bonetti intends to commute to matches from his new home: a guest house on the Isle of Mull. Bonetti only makes seven appearances for the Terrors, and McAlpine is soon back between the sticks on a regular basis.

THURSDAY 23rd JUNE 1904

Willie MacFadyen is born on this day in the mining village of Overtown, near Wishaw in Lanarkshire. After a 15-year playing career at Motherwell – where he won the league – and after serving in the RAF during the Second World War, MacFadyen becomes United manager for a decade from 1945, during which he has an attack-minded team but rarely comes close to achieving promotion.

SATURDAY 24th JUNE 1989

In front of 51,000 fans at Hampden, United's Gary Bollan and Andy McLaren both score for Scotland in the penalty shoot-out after the final of the under-16 World Cup, against Saudi Arabia. Bollan is instrumental in the first half of the match, as Scotland dominate and take a 2-0 lead. Bollan then wins a penalty in the second half, but the Saudi keeper saves Brian O'Neil's spot kick, the bigger, stronger Saudis score twice, and Scotland – which has taken the tournament to its heart – is devastated when their young heroes lose on sudden death in the shoot-out.

THURSDAY 25th JUNE 1970

Paddy Connolly is born on this day in Glasgow. He goes on to become a Scottish under-21 international and establish himself as a regular up front for United in his early 20s. In 1992/93, Connolly is joint top scorer with Duncan Ferguson, before his Tannadice career is curtailed by a series of serious injuries.

SUNDAY 26th JUNE 2011

Boss Peter Houston uses a friendly against Drogheda United, at the start of a pre-season tour in Ireland, as an opportunity to give some youngsters a chance, including Scott Allan, Stuart Armstrong, Ryan Dow and new signing Gary Mackay-Steven. The youthful Tangerines win 2-1, with goals from two more experienced youngsters, Johnny Russell and David Goodwillie.

MONDAY 27th JUNE 1983

John Rankin is born on this day, in Bellshill. When he's 14, he has a brief spell at Tannadice before moving south to the Manchester United youth set-up, and being loaned to Corinthians in Brazil at the age of 18. After that he becomes a key player at Ross County – during which he's capped for the Scotland B team – Inverness Caley Thistle and then Hibs, before returning to Tannadice in 2011, where he becomes a key player in midfield, making 207 appearances and winning the club player of the year award in 2013/14.

THURSDAY 28th JUNE 1984

United sign former Scotland under-21 goalie Billy Thomson for £75,000 from St Mirren. Thomson is initially Hamish McAlpine's understudy but establishes himself as first choice in 1985 – after 37-year-old McAlpine is injured in the League Cup semi-final – and makes 234 appearances for the Terrors. First though, Thomson faces a legal wrangle with St Mirren when he returns to pick up his last pay packet but they try to withhold £200 as a fine for making outspoken remarks about the club.

SATURDAY 29th JUNE 1991

Rachid Bouhenna is born on this day in the small town of Méru, in northern France. In August 2018, big defender Bouhenna – a former Algeria under-23 player – joins United, and features heavily for the season, as the Tangerines chase promotion.

THURSDAY 30th JUNE 1988

United striker Iain Ferguson's Tannadice contract expires. Spanish club Osasuna make an offer to his agent, who also says there's interest from another Spanish club and two French clubs. But the prolific goalscorer ends up at Hearts.

DUNDEE UNITED
ON THIS DAY

JULY

SATURDAY 1st JULY 1967

Dundee United and Aberdeen play a north-east derby, in front of 6,800 fans – in Dallas, as Dallas Tornado and Washington Whips, in the United Soccer Association tournament. The Whips win 2-0 through late goals from Harry Melrose and Jim Whyte.

TUESDAY 2nd JULY 1963

On tour in southern Africa, United lose 2-1 to a Western Province XI in Cape Town, after flying several hundred miles in the morning from their base in Johannesburg. United trainer Andy Dickson had got into trouble in customs when the team arrived in South Africa by trying to take two oranges across the border. He says, 'I caused quite a stir when we arrived here. Apparently they don't like oranges to be brought into the country. I intended eating them on the flight south, but forgot. However, I said I would throw them out. The customs officer must have felt he was asking a Scotsman to do something very much against his grain, because he allowed me through on the promise I would eat them as soon as possible.' United win five, lose two and draw two of their nine matches on the tour.

TUESDAY 3rd JULY 2001

United sign 29-year-old striker Jim McIntyre from Reading. McIntyre – who had had an unsuccessful trial for the Terrors ten years earlier – goes on to score 43 goals in five seasons at Tannadice, including one in the 2005 Scottish Cup semi-final against Hibs.

FRIDAY 4th JULY 2012

Attacking midfielder Michael Gardyne makes his first appearance for United, as they lose a pre-season friendly, 3-0, against Rapid Vienna in Austria. Rapid goalie Lukas Königshofer has to save twice from Gardyne headers in the first half.

TUESDAY 5th JULY 1938

Jimmy Brownlie returns for a third spell as manager, this time accompanied by former Dundee and Northern Ireland player Sam Irving. Brownlie and Irving, who are also directors, are in charge for one season before they step back to the boardroom a year later, when Bobby McKay becomes manager.

TUESDAY 5th JULY 1927

United make a significant signing: 21-year-old centre-forward Duncan Hutchison, who has been released by Dunfermline Athletic because they think he hasn't recovered properly from a broken leg. The transfer comes about as United goalie Bill Paterson – at home in Dunfermline during the summer – hears about Hutchison's quality and convinces Jimmy Brownlie to sign him without seeing him play. That gamble pays off handsomely, as the man who comes to be known as Hurricane Hutch scores 67 goals in his first two seasons and becomes United's first superstar.

MONDAY 5th JULY 1993

United announce Jim McLean's replacement as manager: Ivan Golac. Vice-chairman Doug Smith had been tipped off about Golac by Celtic chairman Jack McGinn, who was impressed by him when he interviewed him for the manager job at Parkhead. After an initial interview in Scotland, Smith and director Bill Littlejohn flew out to Budapest to meet Golac, who travelled 1,400 miles overland from the war-torn former Yugoslavia for the second interview. Unveiling the new boss, Smith says Golac 'is experienced, is confident and has ambition – just like Dundee United – and I think we can work well together.' Golac makes it clear that he's not one for managing expectations when he declares his intention to set his sights high, catch Rangers and 'win the lot', and his first season certainly ends successfully.

MONDAY 6th JULY 1959

Jerry Kerr – who played 28 times for United during the first year of World War II – is appointed as manager at Tannadice. Kerr moves to United from Alloa Athletic, where he was the manager in a part-time capacity, while he also worked as a foreman joiner. *The Evening Telegraph* predicts that he could be the man to put United on the map, and they're right, as, in a 12-year reign, he transforms them from Second Division also-rans into a club firmly established in the top half of the First Division. The United directors had also approached Huddersfield manager Bill Shankly about the job, but he turned them down. He does leave Huddersfield just a few months later though, to take over at Liverpool. And his brother Bob takes a manager's job on Tannadice Street in 1959, as he becomes boss at Dens.

THURSDAY 7th JULY 2005

United sign 31-year-old goalkeeper Derek Stillie from Dunfermline on a two-year contract. Stillie – who is also studying to become a lawyer – is first choice at Tannadice for two seasons, then, at the end of his contract, moves to England to continue his studies.

SATURDAY 8th JULY 1967

Dundee United draw the final match of their first spell as Dallas Tornado, 2-2 with LA Wolves, with the Tornado goals coming from Jackie Graham and a rare Jim Cameron strike. The Tornado finish the tournament bottom of the six-team Western Division, on nine points from 12 games, while the Wolves finish top.

TUESDAY 9th JULY 2002

Seven travelling Arabs fans see United beat Brazilian opposition for the first time, as they defeat Ituano Sao Paulo 2-1 in Austria, in a match that's a friendly only in name. The referee blows for full time after just 85 minutes, having booked four Brazilians and sent one off. Craig Easton says that the provocation from the Brazilian players included spitting. Danny Griffin scores a superb free kick and Stephen O'Donnell gets the winner.

FRIDAY 10th JULY 2015

United lose the first match of a short pre-season tour, 4-0, to Vitesse Arnhem. Mark Durnan and Coll Donaldson make their first appearances for the Terrors in the match, and manager Jackie McNamara says, 'It's our first game [after the summer break] against a quality side, and there are things for us to work on.'

THURSDAY 11th JULY 1991

United sign goalkeeper Guido van de Kamp, to replace the departing Billy Thomson. In three seasons at Tannadice, the moustachioed Dutchman plays 64 times, culminating in the 1994 Scottish Cup Final.

WEDNESDAY 12th JULY 2006

Craig Brewster, making a rare appearance on the pitch during his spell as United player-manager, scores in a pre-season friendly against Herfølge in Denmark. It's his first United goal for over ten years.

*Craig Brewster, the Scottish
Cup goalscoring hero who
returned to Tannadice*

TUESDAY 12th JULY 2011

United sign 21-year-old Gary Mackay-Steven from Airdrie. Manager Peter Houston says: 'He's a winger who has fantastic pace and skill and can deliver great crosses but he still has a lot to learn.' Mackay-Steven – who spent time at Liverpool before picking up an injury and ending up at Airdrie – displays his skill repeatedly during his three and a half seasons at Tannadice, before moving to Celtic.

THURSDAY 13th JULY 2000

On a short pre-season tour in and around Dublin, United beat Bray Wanderers 2-0. Following a defeat to Bohemians in the previous match, manager Paul Sturrock – who is using the tour as an opportunity to experiment with team selection and to check out several trialists – makes nine changes to the team for this game, and Jim Paterson and David Partridge get the only goals. The Tangerines also win their final game of the tour, against St Patrick's Athletic, 2-0.

THURSDAY 14th JULY 2011

United narrowly lose the first leg of their Europa League second qualifying round tie, away against Śląsk Wrocław. Jon Daly fills in in central defence because of injury, while, further forward, Johnny Russell and David Goodwillie miss good chances to open the scoring, before Dutch substitute Johan Voskamp gets the only goal of the game, for the Polish league runners-up, to leave the tie finely balanced.

WEDNESDAY 14th JULY 1993

Duncan Ferguson is transferred to Rangers for £4 million, breaking the transfer record between two British clubs. Manager Ivan Golac is happy with the deal, which gives him the opportunity to bring in new players. He says: 'It was a good board decision with which I was in full agreement, having spoken to both the lad and Mr McLean. Now, maybe, we can concentrate on more important things like getting all the players into the right frame of mind for the start of a long, hard season.' Golac, who has already expressed his interest in Gordan Petrić, adds: 'Whoever we sign will be of international standard and quality and could come either from Scotland or elsewhere.' Craig Brewster joins soon after.

FRIDAY 15th JULY 2016

In Ray McKinnon's first game as United manager, the Terrors become the first ever team to win a League Cup group stage match on penalties. Henri Anier opens the scoring, away against Arbroath, five minutes from the end, but the Red Lichties equalise in the last minute. Under new rules, a penalty shoot-out follows, and when Scott Fraser scores his spot kick, after Cammy Bell saves from Liam Callaghan, United earn an extra point.

SATURDAY 16th JULY 1994

On a hot, humid afternoon in Malaysia, United play in front of at least 80,000 fans in the opening match of an invitational tournament to celebrate the opening of the new Shah Alam stadium, against home side Selangor. Kick-off is delayed by 90 minutes to let the massive crowd in. A Jerren Nixon header hits the bar in the first minute, before Billy McKinlay beats Bruce Grobbelaar – one of five guest players for Selangor – to score the first ever goal at the stadium, in a match that finishes 1-1.

SATURDAY 17th JULY 2004

United beat Burnley 2-1, away, in a pre-season friendly. Barry Robson opens the scoring in the third minute, and 20-year-old defender Mark Wilson sets James Grady up for the winner. After the match, manager Ian McCall says that Wilson's showing why he's becoming one of the most sought-after players in Scotland.

THURSDAY 18th JULY 1996

Craig Brewster, who is out of contract, signs for Greek top-flight side Ionikos, becoming the first player to leave United under the Bosman ruling. He spends five years with Ionikos, where he makes over 150 appearances and scores more than 40 goals.

TUESDAY 19th JULY 2016

Simon Murray gets a hat-trick as United beat Cowdenbeath 6-1 in the League Cup. The Tangerines are 3-0 up after 21 minutes – through Murray, Lewis Toshney and Cammy Smith – before the Blue Brazil pull one back. After Murray gets his second and third – and has another goal ruled out – Henri Anier completes the rout in the dying minutes.

WEDNESDAY 20th JULY 1994

Four days after drawing with Selangor, United play against Bayern Munich in their second match in the invitational tournament in Malaysia, again in suffocating heat. Bayern take the lead early in the second half, but then Ivan Golac brings on new signing Dragutin Ristić, who equalises a few minutes later with a header from a Billy McKinlay cross, but the draw puts the German side into the final of the tournament.

THURSDAY 21st JULY 2011

At a packed Tannadice, United beat Śląsk Wrocław 3-2 in a dramatic Europa League qualifying match but go out on away goals. Keith Watson and David Goodwillie give the Terrors a 2-0 lead after just five minutes, sparking a mini pitch invasion from delighted fans. The Polish side get an important away goal just ten minutes after that, but, when Goodwillie is brought down just before the break, Jon Daly restores the Tangerines' aggregate lead from the penalty spot. But a second-half goal from Sebastian Dudek puts Śląsk in the driving seat again, and although United pour forward, and Daly hits the bar in injury time, the men from Tannadice are out.

THURSDAY 22nd JULY 1999

A Newcastle team including the likes of Gary Speed and Temuri Ketsbaia visit Tannadice as part of Dundee United's 90th anniversary celebrations, and the Tangerines enjoy the party, beating the Magpies 3-1 with goals from Billy Dodds, Jim Paterson and Siggi Jónsson.

WEDNESDAY 23rd JULY 1997

Andy McLaren is involved in five of United's goals as the Terrors win 8-0 away in the UEFA Cup qualifying round, against Principat in Andorra. Robbie Winters scores four, Gary McSwegan gets three and Lars Zetterlund scores once and misses a penalty, but boss Tommy McLean refuses to get carried away, saying 'there was lots of ragged play out there and there remains a lot of improving to be done'. And he follows that up with words that the amateurs from Andorra probably don't want to hear: 'It would be disrespectful to Principat if we fielded a team of kids [in the second leg]. We'll put out as strong a side as we possibly can.'

Scottish Cup-winning manager Ivan Golac. Never a dull moment.

SUNDAY 24th JULY 2005

In the final of the inaugural City of Discovery Cup, United come from behind to beat Sheffield Wednesday 2-1 and win the trophy, with Garry Kenneth getting the winning goal five minutes from the end. The day before, United had knocked out Dundee in their semi-final in the four-team tournament, which lasts for just two seasons.

THURSDAY 25th JULY 2013

United sign 21-year-old Turkish striker Nadir Çiftçi. Manager Jackie McNamara says Çiftçi 'is strong and clever and has pace and an eye for goal', and the young Turk proves his boss right by being the club's top scorer in his two seasons at Tannadice, before United sell him to Celtic for £1.5 million.

THURSDAY 26th JULY 2007

Barcelona, who have been doing pre-season training in St Andrews, finally pluck up the courage to return to Tannadice, the scene of repeated previous azulgrana heartache, this time for a glamour friendly. In the last minute in a packed stadium, Thierry Henry scores the only goal of the game, his first for the Catalan giants. The global stars who take on the Terrors include Gianluca Zambrotta, Lilian Thuram, Xavi, Andrés Iniesta, Yaya Touré, Samuel Eto'o, Ronaldinho and Deco. At half-time, United players who beat Barcelona in 1966 and 1987 are paraded on the pitch, and after the match Barça boss Frank Rijkaard says, 'It seemed like more than a friendly. It was aggressive and had rhythm,' and adds: 'Dundee United played well and maybe deserved one and we created a lot of chances. It was a good test.' United boss Craig Levein says, 'I need a new striker. Frank seems to have a few; I'll maybe ask him for one.'

SATURDAY 26th JULY 2008

Barcelona return to the city of discovery, one year on, for another friendly. Prince Buaben sends the crowd wild when he gives the Terrors the lead but Thierry Henry soon equalises from a Dani Alves cross, and Barça – two days after beating Hibs 6-0 at Murrayfield – score four without reply in the second half, through Samuel Eto'o and 21-year-old substitute Lionel Messi, who gets three.

SUNDAY 26th JULY 2015

Dutch midfielder Rodney Sneijder – global star Wesley's younger brother – signs for United on a two-year deal. Manager Jackie McNamara says: 'He has a fabulous pedigree and you can see his talent. He will become a fans' favourite at Tannadice and this signing is a real coup for the club.' Sneijder makes one appearance as a substitute, in a 1-0 defeat to Aberdeen, but unfortunately he falls ill and is released from his contract one month after signing. United offer to replace any shirts that fans have bought with his famous name on the back.

SATURDAY 27th JULY 2013

Two days after signing for United, Nadir Çiftçi blasts home a shot from 25 yards to score the only goal of the game, in a pre-season friendly away to FA Cup holders Wigan. The Turkish striker says, 'It's my best goal ever. I just decided to try my luck and thankfully it went in. It's been a dream week for me having just joined the club.' Jackie McNamara says: 'Nadir has got that in his locker. I didn't think he was having his best game and then he goes and produces that kind of goal. That's why we've signed him and we've all got high hopes for him.'

SATURDAY 28th JULY 1979

Shortly after being named SPFA Young Player of the Year, teenage full-back Ray Stewart scores his last goal for United, at Hampden, in the Dryburgh Cup semi-final against Celtic. A month later he moves to West Ham for £400,000, breaking the record for a defender transferred from a Scottish club. Stewart goes on to score 60 goals for West Ham, while United use the transfer fee to pay for ground improvements and Eamonn Bannon.

WEDNESDAY 29th JULY 1998

Roughly 3,000 fans turn out in pouring rain on a Wednesday afternoon to watch Dundee United play against Dundee United, in a public trial match between the first team and the reserve team. The reserves are 2-0 up after 13 minutes, through goals from 19-year-old Steven Thompson and Gary McSwegan, but the first team come back to win 4-2.

WEDNESDAY 30th JULY 1997

United record a club record 17-0 aggregate win as they thump Principat again, 9-0, in the home leg of their UEFA Cup tie. Gary McSwegan gets a hat-trick, Robbie Winters scores twice and the other goals are shared out between Andy McLaren, Kjell Olofsson, Lars Zetterlund and teenager Steven Thompson, with his first goal for the club. Maurice Malpas and Dave Bowman both miss late chances as the Terrors miss out on equalling the record aggregate victory by a Scottish club in Europe by one goal. Principat coach Manolo Marin says, 'Dundee United are the best team we have played in our history.'

WEDNESDAY 31st JULY 1991

More than 12,000 fans turn out for Maurice Malpas's testimonial, as United beat a full-strength Rangers side 3-1, in what Jim McLean describes as one of the best testimonial matches he's seen. The Tangerines are 2-0 up after five minutes, through Hamish French and Michael O'Neill, and French strikes again to make it 3-0 at the break. A decade later, Malpas earns another testimonial, against Everton.

DUNDEE UNITED
ON THIS DAY

AUGUST

SUNDAY 1st AUGUST 1982

Eight thousand fans turn up at Tannadice on a Sunday evening for a friendly between United and West Ham, and they're rewarded with an entertaining match between two quality sides. Twenty-year-old Alex Taylor, who was impressive in friendlies in Scandinavia in July, sets Davie Dodds up for the opening goal, but François Van der Elst and Paul Goddard put the Hammers in front by half-time. Paul Sturrock equalises early in the second half, before Geoff Pike restores the Londoners' lead and then Dodds makes the final score 3-3. *The Evening Telegraph* reports that that 20-year-old United 'action man' Richard Gough is more eye-catching than his opposite number, former Tannadice prodigy Ray Stewart.

MONDAY 2nd AUGUST 1937

Jim Yuill McLean is born on this day in Larkhall, to religious parents Tom and Annie. Tom, a baker, had been a junior footballer until he married Annie, whose father, William Yuille – who played for Rangers before the First World War – was strictly religious. Tom joined the Plymouth Brethren when he married into the family, which meant no more football – playing or watching – as well as no alcohol, cinema or TV. Jim – who remains teetotal throughout his life – and his brothers Willie and Tommy all go on to become footballers, with dad Tom unable to watch them play, but proud of their achievements. Jim serves an apprenticeship as a joiner and plays for Hamilton, Clyde, Dundee and Kilmarnock – in spite of suffering from a lack of self-confidence – before becoming a coach at Dens Park, then being offered the manager job at Tannadice, where he's a huge success.

SATURDAY 2nd AUGUST 1969

Inspired by the colours they wore when they were playing as Dallas Tornado in the USA, United play in their new strip – of tangerine shirts and shorts with black trim – in the UK for the first time, in a friendly away to Everton. Ian Scott opens the scoring for the visitors but Everton – who, according to *The Evening Telegraph*, are 'just too fruity for the Tangerines' – win 4-1, with goals from Jimmy Husband, John Hurst, Colin Harvey and Joe Royle. Royle is so dominant in the air that the *Tele* says he keeps 'taking off like a jump jet'.

FRIDAY 2nd AUGUST 2013

Six new United players – Andy Robertson, Nadir Çiftçi, Paul Paton, Calum Butcher and substitutes Chris Erskine and Brian Graham – make their competitive debuts, in the first league match of the season, a 0-0 draw away to Partick Thistle. Robertson plays particularly well in a match full of chances but where both keepers make several good saves.

WEDNESDAY 3rd AUGUST 2011

David Goodwillie moves to Blackburn Rovers for a deal worth between £2 million and £3 million, following several rejected bids from Rangers for the 22-year-old striker. Blackburn boss Steve Kean says, 'David has always been put on a parallel with a young Wayne Rooney and you can see that when you see him play.' But Goodwillie fails to establish himself in England, and returns to Tannadice on loan two years later.

SUNDAY 4th AUGUST 1991

United get their best result from a short pre-season tour in the Netherlands, as they beat regional second division side Veloc Eindhoven 6-2. The Dutch side score first with an early penalty but Michael O'Neill and Ray McKinnon both score twice and Darren Jackson and Hamish French get one each.

SATURDAY 5th AUGUST 2000

United lose 3-0 to Hibs, and manager Paul Sturrock tells chairman Jim McLean and the players that he's resigning. Two days later he makes it official and the club reluctantly accept his resignation. Sturrock goes on to manage clubs in England, and, in 2018, briefly becomes United's chief scout in England, and then a temporary coach at Tannadice.

SUNDAY 6th AUGUST 1995

Dave Bowman has to get special dispensation from the SFA to play in his own testimonial – a Dundee derby – after being suspended for four matches at the end of the previous season. The United team features several young players, and 17-year-old winger Paul Walker comes on as a substitute and sets up the winning goal for Craig Brewster, in a 2-1 victory. *The Evening Telegraph* reports that Bowman turns in a 'typically solid' performance.

SUNDAY 6th AUGUST 1989

United beat Real Sociedad 1-0 in Paul Sturrock's testimonial. At the age of 41, Hamish McAlpine returns to the team when he comes on as a substitute in the second half, to loud cheers from the crowd. New signing Freddy van der Hoorn impresses in his first home appearance, playing at left-back, which enables Jim McLean to move Maurice Malpas into midfield. The only goal of the game comes from a van der Hoorn long ball, which young defender Iñaki Álaba turns into his own net.

SUNDAY 7th AUGUST 1988

A strong Tottenham side – including a young Paul Gascoigne, shortly after he signed from Newcastle – provide the opposition for Dave Narey's testimonial on a sunny day at Tannadice. *The Evening Telegraph* reports that both teams 'showed plenty of evidence that they are teams to be reckoned with. The number of quality players on view was dazzling, with Paul Walsh a real crowd-pleaser for the visitors.' United take the lead through Alex Cleland, before, unfortunately, a clearance ricochets off of Narey and into his own goal. The match finishes 1-1, and Narey ruefully says afterwards that it isn't how he'd wanted to score in his own testimonial.

WEDNESDAY 8th AUGUST 1984

Brian Clough brings his Nottingham Forest side to Tannadice for Jim McLean's testimonial – which was arranged shortly after the manager turned down a move to Rangers – and gives his son Nigel his debut in the match, but it's United's Ralph Milne who steals the show, scoring two goals – both set up by Paul Sturrock – as the Tangerines win 2-0. Milne and Eamonn Bannon both come close to scoring again in the second half. *The Glasgow Herald* describes Milne's goals as sensational and says that United play some clever one-touch football, completely outclassing Forest.

THURSDAY 9th AUGUST 2012

In their last game in Europe to date, United suffer a painful away day as they lose 5-0 in the Europa League qualifying rounds to Dynamo Moscow – who are playing their first match under a new manager – and go out 7-2 on aggregate.

TUESDAY 9th AUGUST 1977

United take on a Doug Smith Select in Doug Smith's testimonial. Stalwart heroic defender Smith scores a penalty in the match, but his side, which includes stars like Bobby Lennox, Ron Yeats, Finn Døssing, Mogens Berg, Roy Aitken, Tommy McLean and Willie Miller, loses 5-4 to a United side in which youngsters Paul Sturrock, Billy Kirkwood and Graeme Payne all impress. At full time Smith is carried off the pitch on the other players' shoulders. Lennox describes the game as 'the best of its type I've ever played in. Perfectly friendly but very competitive.'

SATURDAY 10th AUGUST 1935

The Evening Telegraph reports that Duncan Hutchison's 'generalship was just grand' as he plays in his first game in his second spell at United, a 2-2 draw with St Bernard's, after spending five years playing in England with Newcastle, Derby and Hull.

SATURDAY 11th AUGUST 1962

Dundee are the first visitors to the 'new' Tannadice following the construction of the new L-shaped main stand, which is the third ever stand with a cantilevered roof to be built at a British football stadium. *The Evening Telegraph* says: 'Here is one of the finest stadiums in the country. Here, too, is the nucleus of a team that can put United on the road to a great season,' as the home side beat the league champions 3-2.

TUESDAY 12th AUGUST 1997

Eleven United fans make a pilgrimage to Turkey to see United take on Trabzonspor in a UEFA Cup first-leg match. The Terrors play well but lose 1-0 to the Turks, who have five internationals in their team, through a late penalty, leaving manager Tommy McLean optimistic about the home leg. The match is played on such a hot and humid evening that it's estimated that the players lose half a stone on average, so they're given a two-litre bottle of Coke each to drink after the match. *The Evening Telegraph* reports that 'United were promised as hostile an atmosphere as they had ever come across', but that 'few of the small band of United fans who travelled could remember a friendlier opposing support'.

SATURDAY 13th AUGUST 1927

Duncan Hutchison makes an impressive goalscoring debut for United, in a 4-2 home win over Bathgate. *The Evening Telegraph* says that 'Hutchison earned the biggest "plum". His football was fiery, his bullets were never far removed from their billet, and he was a continual source of worry to opposing defenders.' As well as scoring, Hutchison fires in a left-foot shot that 'gave the crossbar something to think about, and removed the paint'.

SATURDAY 13th AUGUST 1966

Billy Hainey becomes the first Dundee United player to come on as a substitute, replacing injured Dennis Gillespie and scoring, in a 2-0 defeat of Dundee. The substitution is an inconvenience for Middlesbrough, who've sent a scout to watch Gillespie.

SATURDAY 14th AUGUST 1943

United beat Hearts 6-3 at Tannadice on the opening day of the season, with Albert Juliussen getting a hat-trick for the home side. *The Evening Telegraph*'s 'Rambler' reports that United debutants Charlie McDermott, Geo Thomson, Percy Bower and John Wilson all play well, with Bower among the goals. But due to the nature of wartime football, none of the debutants stays at Tannadice for long, especially Bower. It's his only game for United.

SATURDAY 15th AUGUST 1925

The Courier reports that United are 'far from disgraced' as they play their first ever game in Division One, away to Raith Rovers in August sunshine, on the first day of the new offside rule. United are 3-0 down at half-time, but improve after the break, with Jimmy Howieson getting United's first two top-flight goals, and the 4-2 final score is – according to *The Courier* – a fair reflection of the game.

WEDNESDAY 16th AUGUST 1989

Two days after signing from Newcastle for a club record fee of £350,000, 20-year-old wide midfielder Michael O'Neill makes a goalscoring debut, getting the only goal of the game against Partick, 'dummying his way into the danger area in style', according to *The Glasgow Herald*, 'before crashing the winner past the advancing [Andy] Murdoch.'

SATURDAY 16th AUGUST 1941

Albert Juliussen scores twice on his debut for United, playing as a trialist in a 4-1 win away against St Bernard's in the wartime North Eastern League, with United's other goals both coming from Cornelius Holland. *The Evening Telegraph*'s 'Rambler' reports that, if things go as expected, Juliussen will be a regular in the United team in the future. Rambler's right. Juliussen – who seems prepared to shoot from anywhere – scores 89 goals for United in 76 matches during the war, as well as drawing countless saves from keepers and regularly smashing the ball against the posts and bar.

WEDNESDAY 16th AUGUST 1967

United thrash Aberdeen 5-0 in the group stages of the League Cup at Tannadice, with all of the goals coming in the second half. *The Press and Journal*'s Norman MacDonald reports that the 'home team gave a magnificent second half display and few teams would have survived against them'. Finn Seemann scores twice, with Billy Hainey, Davie Wilson and Dennis Gillespie getting the others.

WEDNESDAY 17th AUGUST 1983

A strong Tottenham side – including Ossie Ardiles, Glenn Hoddle, Gary Mabbutt and Steve Archibald – comes to Tannadice for Hamish McAlpine's testimonial, which *The Glasgow Herald* describes as a feast of football. Tony Galvin finishes off a good move to open the scoring for the visitors, before John Clark heads an equaliser past Ray Clemence. In the second half, McAlpine makes great saves from Archibald and Micky Hazard before 21-year-old United substitute Alex Taylor hits the underside of the crossbar from 25 yards and Clemence saves well from Billy Kirkwood, as the match finishes 1-1.

SUNDAY 17th AUGUST 1986

Richard Gough is transferred for £750,000 to Tottenham, who've been impressed by his performances for Scotland at the World Cup in Mexico. United weren't keen to sell him, and Jim McLean isn't happy about it, since Gough is still under contract, but the defender wanted to move, amid interest from several clubs, including Rangers, Everton, Chelsea and Manchester United. McLean is flabbergasted when Gough asks him for advice on whether he should choose Spurs or Chelsea.

WEDNESDAY 18th AUGUST 1909

Dundee Hibs play their first ever game, a friendly against Hibs, in front of at least 6,000 fans at Tannadice, which was, before Dundee Hibs rebuilt it, known as Clepington Park. Dundee Hibs have had to quickly build a new pavilion, terracings and fence, after the previous tenants, Dundee Wanderers, who were unhappy about being evicted, removed the existing stand, dressing rooms, goals and fence. The match finishes 1-1, with the Edinburgh side's John O'Hara scoring the first ever goal in a Dundee Hibs match, while Jamie Docherty scores the first ever – and his only – goal for the home side. Dundee Hibs supremo – and bike shop owner – Pat Reilly gives O'Hara a bike as a reward for his opening goal.

SATURDAY 18th AUGUST 1923

As part of their attempts to appeal to a wider fan base, Dundee Hibs play in their new, non-Irish strip for the first time. The team, who previously played in green shirts and white shorts, line up for the first game of the season, against Cowdenbeath, in front of 10,000 supporters at Tannadice in their new colours of white shirts and black shorts. Although the match – the first under manager Jimmy Brownlie – finishes 0-0, *The Evening Telegraph* reports that the home side were far superior to Cowdenbeath and that they should be one of the season's 'big guns' in the Second Division.

WEDNESDAY 18th AUGUST 1976

Seventeen-year-old striker Davie Dodds scores twice on his United debut, away to Arbroath in the League Cup. Arbroath goalie Gordon Marshall – the father of future Celtic and Scotland goalie Gordon Marshall – makes four great saves in the first half, and Dodds' and United's first goal – hammered home from a perfectly delivered low ball from Paul Sturrock – comes an hour into the match, five minutes after the Red Lichties had opened the scoring, and shortly after *The Evening Telegraph*'s match reporter agreed with the man next to him that 'young Dodds, though ever brave and willing, was somewhat out of his depth'. But confident Dodds' rampant last half-hour and his second goal of the match convince the *Tele*'s man that he 'has the makings all right', as the Tangerines win 3-1, with Sturrock adding the last goal.

High-scoring striker Davie Dodds, who started as he meant to go on

SATURDAY 18th AUGUST 1917

The first ever Dundee league derby – in the wartime Eastern League – finishes 5-1 to the home team, at Dens Park, but *The Courier* reports that, 'The Hibs were by no means outplayed; indeed, the score is perhaps just a little more flattering to Dundee than they deserve.'

MONDAY 19th AUGUST 1935

One week after drawing with First Division Dundee at home, Second Division United endure a painful Forfarshire Cup semi-final replay against their local rivals at Dens Park, as they lose 8-1. To add insult to injury, Arthur Milne has a penalty saved, before he grabs United's consolation goal two minutes from the end.

SATURDAY 20th AUGUST 1910

Dundee Hibs play their first ever Second Division match, at home to Leith Athletic, but lose 3-2, with *The Courier* reporting that the home side are unlucky to lose, that the team is 'in some parts exceptionally good', and that, once the players know each other better, they should do well in the league. Left-winger John Collins – one of the players given special praise by *The Courier* – gets the Tannadice side's first two league goals.

MONDAY 20th AUGUST 1923

As they continue their attempts to appeal to more potential fans, Dundee Hibs decide, at their AGM, to change their name to Dundee City, but Dundee object to the change, saying that each club's mail could be accidentally delivered to the wrong stadium because of it. The decision on whether to allow the name change will go to a vote between SFA members a month later.

TUESDAY 21st AUGUST 1990

Sixteen-year-old striker Christian Dailly scores on his Dundee United debut, a 3-0 away win at Alloa in the League Cup, and also goes on to score in the next two games, at the start of an impressive career, during which he moves from attack back to defence. He's particularly successful during his spells at United, Blackburn and West Ham, and he makes 67 appearances for Scotland, including 12 as captain.

SATURDAY 21st AUGUST 1909

In the season before they are elected to the Second Division, Dundee Hibs play for a year in the Northern League. On this day, they play their first ever league match, at home to Dundee Wanderers, a few weeks after controversially taking over their Tannadice tenancy. Hibs lose 2-1, but *The Courier* reports that they're unlucky and that their forward line 'played a fine passing game, but their shooting at close quarters could have been improved upon'. Joe Hannan scores Dundee Hibs' first ever competitive goal, but also misses a penalty.

WEDNESDAY 22nd AUGUST 2007

United midfielder Barry Robson makes his Scotland debut, as a substitute against South Africa at Pittodrie, and clears a Thembinkosi Fanteni header off the line late on in a 1-0 victory for the Scots. Robson goes on to play for Scotland 16 more times.

SATURDAY 23rd AUGUST 1941

United winger James Witherspoon informs the club that he'll be unable to get leave to play against Aberdeen in the wartime North Eastern League on this day, but then unexpectedly becomes available. He turns up at Tannadice but his position has been taken by John Ross, who scores in the first minute as, according to 'Rambler' in *The Evening Telegraph*, the home side make a 'sad hash of the more fancied Aberdeen team'. Ross scores another, Cornelius Holland gets two, and Albert Juliussen scores one, as United win 5-0.

WEDNESDAY 24th AUGUST 1960

In their first Division One match since 1932, United – who have gone full-time again following their promotion – beat Hibs 3-1. In the first 15 minutes, Eric Walker and Tommy McLeod both score and United have another goal ruled out. Ron Yeats keeps Hibs' star centre-forward Joe Baker under control, while new goalie Lando Ugolini makes some good saves as the Terrors make an impressive return to the top flight.

WEDNESDAY 24th AUGUST 1954

Following three straight defeats in the League Cup group stage, United manager Willie MacFadyen shocks the Tannadice board by resigning.

THURSDAY 25th AUGUST 2005

In the second leg of their UEFA Cup tie against MyPa 47, United seem to be cruising into the next round, as they lead 2-0 – on the night and on aggregate – at Tannadice with 20 minutes left to play. The Tangerines spurn chances to stretch the lead and, after 74 minutes, the Finnish side win a penalty, which Brazilian Adriano slots home. Seven minutes later, Adriano gets his second. United throw everything at the visitors, but Barry Robson and Paul Ritchie miss late chances and United go out on away goals.

TUESDAY 26th AUGUST 1997

United can't quite do enough to overturn Trabzonspor's 1-0 lead from the away leg of their UEFA Cup tie. Andy McLaren heads a Lars Zetterlund cross past goalie Metin Aktaş early in the second half at Tannadice, and Gary McSwegan draws an impressive save from the young keeper, but Hami gets the vital away goal ten minutes from the end to knock the Tangerines out 2-1 on aggregate. Before the match, Trabzonspor coach Yilmaz Vural had said that, on the evidence of the first leg, United were ten years behind his side tactically, but after the draw Tommy McLean says, 'We showed there maybe isn't a lot wrong with Scottish football if we can play like that. They talked about being ten years ahead, but a lot of people in their camp must be relieved as they could easily have gone out.'

THURSDAY 26th AUGUST 2010

United play AEK Athens in the second leg of their Europa League play-off, at the home ground of Olympiacos. Because of problems with the pitch at AEK's ground, the game had been moved to Panionios's stadium, but Panionios fans sabotaged their own pitch so that the venue had to be changed again. Five hundred Arabs make it to the right venue, to see the Tangerines almost do enough to overturn a 1-0 defeat from the home leg. AEK stretch their aggregate lead on the night, but Jon Daly knocks home a Paul Dixon cross in the 78th minute and Danny Swanson comes close to getting a decisive second away goal near the end, but it finishes 1-1 and United go out 2-1 on aggregate.

TUESDAY 27th AUGUST 1929

United's star striker Duncan Hutchison is sold to Newcastle for £4,000, as Jimmy Brownlie and United's chairman William Hutchison and director A B Carnegie negotiate the deal with Newcastle representatives at Edinburgh's North British Hotel. The fee is large but unhappy fans protest outside Tannadice. One 'ex-Dundee United supporter' writes to *The Evening Telegraph* to lament the 'hairy hoof of finance that obtrudes itself'.

SATURDAY 27th AUGUST 1949

United beat Airdrie 6-0 in the League Cup group stage at Tannadice. George Cruickshank and Peter McKay score in the first half, and – in a deadly five-minute period just after the break – McKay gets another while Frank Quinn scores two. McKay completes his hat-trick ten minutes from the end, as, *The Courier* says, 'the 16,000 cheering fans saw their team move with machine-like precision'.

SATURDAY 28th AUGUST 1909

Dundee Hibs earn their first win in the Northern League, beating Montrose 1-0 through a goal from winger Henry Brown. *The Evening Telegraph* says the match is 'a good, hard tussle' and that Hibs are good value for the points.

SATURDAY 29th AUGUST 1925

United play their first ever home game in Division One, against Falkirk, on the day when the Second Division championship flag is unfurled at an extended and improved Tannadice. Willie Oswald opens the scoring for the home side, but Falkirk equalise just before half-time and get another in the last minute, to win 2-1, with *The Courier* reporting that United are unlucky to take nothing from the game.

WEDNESDAY 29th AUGUST 1973

At the age of 17, Andy Gray scores his first goal for United, with a superb header in his second appearance, in a 5-2 defeat of East Fife in the League Cup. *The Glasgow Herald* describes Gray and Graeme Payne – who's also 17 – as outstanding. The Tangerines' other goals come from Kenny Cameron, Walter Smith, Duncan MacLeod and a Doug Smith penalty, while Paul Hegarty's big brother Kevin gets one of East Fife's goals.

FRIDAY 30th AUGUST 2019

Before the first Dundee derby of the season kicks off, on a Friday night at a sold-out Tannadice, United boss Robbie Neilson says: 'It'll be 100 miles per hour for the first 95 minutes and then it'll settle down.' He's pretty much right. The Tangerines are 4-1 up at half time and add a fifth two minutes after the break, in a game that finishes 6-2 to the home side. Calum Butcher scores twice, and Louis Appere, Lawrence Shankland, Ian Harkes and Cammy Smith get one each. Shankland's strike is his tenth in his first eight games for the Terrors, and the result leaves United top of the Championship table with a 100% record, seven points ahead of their local rivals after just four games.

SATURDAY 31st AUGUST 1929

The first match after Duncan Hutchison's controversial transfer to Newcastle is the Dundee derby at Dens Park. United fans organise a boycott, and the attendance is 6,000 lower than the previous league meeting at Dens. A group of United fans even organise coaches to take them to Newcastle to cheer on Hutchison, and some of them present him with a lucky horseshoe before the match. The stay-away fans don't miss much at Dens Park, as Dundee win a poor game, in poor conditions and on a sodden pitch, 1-0. Writing in *The Courier*, 'The Laird' predicts that United will need reinforcements if they're to do well in the First Division. Centre-forward George Thomson, who's been bought from Clydebank as Hutchison's replacement, doesn't make much of an impression, and he leaves Tannadice at the end of the season, after scoring just two goals.

DUNDEE UNITED

ON THIS DAY

SEPTEMBER

SUNDAY 1st SEPTEMBER 1958

Billy Kirkwood is born on this day in Edinburgh. When he's 17, he joins United and becomes a key player in the Tangerines' most successful era, playing 399 times for the club in ten years and scoring 70 goals. A versatile midfielder, he plays in 31 of the 36 league matches in the title-winning season and features regularly on big European nights.

WEDNESDAY 2nd SEPTEMBER 1981

League Cup holders Dundee United beat Hamilton 4-0 away in their League Cup quarter-final first leg. *The Glasgow Herald* reports that the Terrors turned in a thrilling display, with Paul Sturrock in particular 'a constant thorn in the Hamilton defence, threatening danger every time he had possession'. Davie Dodds scores twice with headers in the first 20 minutes. After the break, Sturrock sets up John Holt for the third. Less than 60 seconds later, Sturrock is pulled down in the penalty area, and Eamonn Bannon blasts home the spot kick.

SATURDAY 3rd SEPTEMBER 1983

United secure their 11th consecutive win in competitive matches, and their sixth consecutive defeat of Dundee, beating their local rivals 4-1 at Dens Park. Twenty-one-year-old John 'Boney' Reilly – deputising for injured Paul Sturrock – scores twice, while Dundee goalie Colin Kelly also has to make two top-class saves from the stand-in striker, whose performance Jim McLean describes as 'magnificent'. Ralph Milne and Derek Stark add United's other goals, in the last 15 minutes of the game.

SATURDAY 4th SEPTEMBER 1909

Dundee Hibs hire their first ever special train, which takes 1,000 fans to Brechin for a Qualifying Cup tie. *The Courier* describes the match as one of the best ever played in Brechin, and says that, with the home side 2-1 up, 'in the closing 15 minutes Hibs pressed, and pressed severely, for an equalising goal. They lashed to the right of them; they lashed to the left of them; they lashed in front of them; they tried cute, close-in play; and all the time the big crowd was brimming over with excitement.' But the home side hold on to their narrow lead.

WEDNESDAY 5th SEPTEMBER 1984

United beat Celtic 2-1 after extra time in a dramatic League Cup quarter-final in front of 21,000 fans at Tannadice. In a fast-paced end-to-end game, the opening goal comes in the second half when Paul Sturrock fires a low shot past Pat Bonner, following an Eamonn Bannon free kick. Alan McInally equalises less than ten minutes from the end to send the game into extra time, when teenage substitute John Clark's low drive sends the Terrors into the semi-final.

WEDNESDAY 6th SEPTEMBER 1961

Inside-forward Dennis Gillespie becomes the first Dundee United player to play for the Scottish League, in a 1-1 draw with the League of Ireland in Dublin. Gillespie – who scores 115 goals in 12 years with the Terrors – is involved in the build-up for Scotland's only goal of the game, scored by another debutant, Celtic's John Hughes.

SATURDAY 7th SEPTEMBER 1996

United lose Billy Kirkwood's last game in charge as manager, 1-0 to Hearts at Tannadice. With Kirkwood's side having taken just one point from their first four league games of their first season back in the Premier Division, the boss is replaced in the dug-out by Tommy McLean.

MONDAY 8th SEPTEMBER 1947

United sign 24-year-old centre-forward Peter McKay from junior side Newburgh, where he's scored 16 goals in his first five games, in his first season as a footballer, after serving in the RAF during World War II. United manager Willie MacFadyen visits the Fife club to seal the deal, just a few hours before St Johnstone boss Jimmy Crapnell turns up with the same idea. McKay becomes a United superstar, scoring 203 goals in 241 appearances, before he joins Burnley in 1954.

SATURDAY 8th SEPTEMBER 1979

At the age of 18, Ralph Milne scores in his first league match, after coming on as a substitute, and Willie Pettigrew gets his first United goal, from the penalty spot, as United draw 2-2 with league champions Celtic at Parkhead.

WEDNESDAY 9th SEPTEMBER 1964

In a League Cup quarter-final first leg that *The Glasgow Herald* describes as 'a painful case of class distinction in football', four United players – Frannie Munro, Ian Mitchell, Jimmy McManus and Lewis Thom – get two goals each as the Terrors stick eight past Hamilton, with seven of the goals coming in the first half. A week later, only 620 fans turn up for the away leg, which United win 2-1, to make the aggregate score 10-1.

SATURDAY 10th SEPTEMBER 1949

With Arsenal representative Tommy Cairns watching from the Tannadice stand, United beat Alloa 6-1. Surprisingly, star centre-forward Peter McKay only scores once, but he also sets up three of United's four first half goals. Jim Elliot and George Grant each score twice, and Emilio Pacione – in as a late replacement for injured George Cruickshank – gets the other.

SATURDAY 11th SEPTEMBER 1965

Jim McLean makes his Dundee debut in the Dens Park Massacre: United's record victory in the derby, 5-0 at Dens Park. Finn Døssing scores a hat-trick, Lennart Wing gets his first goal for United, from the penalty spot, and Dennis Gillespie grabs the other as the Terrors humiliate their local rivals.

TUESDAY 11th SEPTEMBER 1990

Sixteen-year-old United striker Christian Dailly becomes the youngest ever player to play for the Scotland under-21 team, as he plays from the start in a 2-0 win against Romania at Easter Road. Dailly goes on to earn a record 34 caps for the under-21s.

SATURDAY 12th SEPTEMBER 1925

After taking just one point from their first five Division One league games, United earn their first ever top-flight victory on this day, 1-0 away to St Johnstone, through a Peter McMillan goal. There's late drama as United goalie Bill Paterson secures the victory with a brilliant save from a Saints free kick, but bangs his head on the post and is laid out. Meanwhile, McMillan only plays for United two more times, without scoring again.

Christian Dailly's talent was clear from an early age, for United and Scotland

SATURDAY 12th SEPTEMBER 1959

United beat Queen's Park 8-1, away, in the league. The Spiders take the lead from the penalty spot, but, with Ron Yeats dictating play, Jim Irvine scores twice before half-time. And in the second half United take total control and score six more. Irvine takes his total to four, while Dennis Gillespie gets a second-half hat-trick and Watt Newton scores once.

WEDNESDAY 13th SEPTEMBER 1978

As United are on their way home from a UEFA Cup away leg against Standard Liege, Jim McLean is livid at Brussels airport when Derby County assistant manager Frank Blunstone approaches Dave Narey. Derby boss Tommy Docherty has already revealed that he's interested in signing Narey, and McLean makes it clear to Blunstone that he shouldn't be talking to his player. Later, Blunstone says, 'It was just a casual chat with a group of lads, but Jim McLean burst out of the duty free shop and started prodding me on the chest and bellowing. I've never tapped up a player in my life and if I was going to start with Narey I'd have more sense than to try it in an airport lounge surrounded by players, directors and press men. It was a bad trip all round. The game was switched from Liege to Ghent without my knowing, so I only saw the second half. I lost a £70 raincoat on the flight to Brussels, and then got involved in a public slanging match through no fault of my own.' The price of the raincoat isn't the only unexpected cost that Blunstone incurs on his trip. He's fined £500 after United complain to the SFA about his approach to Narey.

WEDNESDAY 14th SEPTEMBER 1983

John Reilly scores United's first ever European Cup goal just two minutes into their match against Hamrun Spartans in Malta. The Tangerines take to the pitch – which Jim McLean later describes as 'baked hard by the sun and scorched by deep ruts made by tractors' – straight after Rangers, who were playing Valletta in the European Cup Winners' Cup at the same venue. The Maltese players repeatedly foul their opponents, but United win comfortably, with Ralph Milne and Derek Stark getting goals number two and three.

MONDAY 15th SEPTEMBER 1969

United return to the Fairs Cup two years after beating Barcelona, and are drawn against the holders again, as Newcastle visit Tannadice for the first leg of their first-round tie. The Magpies' Wyn Davies is a constant threat in the air, hitting the bar three times from headers in the first half, and giving the visitors a 2-0 lead, with two more headers, after the break. Things get worse when the Terrors' goalkeeper, Don Mackay, is injured in a collision with Newcastle's Tommy Gibb and has to be replaced by 19-year-old Ged Reilly, a recent signing from Montrose who's making his only ever appearance for the Tangerines. But the home side go on the attack, and Ian Scott pulls one back from a header, and it's the visitors who have to defend for the last 15 minutes, to hold on to their 2-1 lead, ahead of the return leg two weeks later.

TUESDAY 15th SEPTEMBER 1970

In their third season in the Fairs Cup, United pull off a dramatic late comeback to beat Swiss side Grasshoppers 3-2 in the first round, first leg at Tannadice. After their goalie Rene Deck pulls off three good saves in the first seven minutes, the visitors take a surprise two-goal lead through Sweden international Ove Grahn and Peter Meier, two of three players who Jerry Kerr singled out for praise before the match. But Ian Reid pulls one back for United midway through the second half, Stuart Markland equalises ten minutes from the end, and Alec Reid gets the winner in the last minute. In Switzerland two weeks later, United survive two late scares to draw 0-0 and win on aggregate in Europe for the second ever time.

WEDNESDAY 15th SEPTEMBER 1982

PSV Eindhoven goalie Pim Doesburg makes great saves from Maurice Malpas, Davie Dodds, Paul Sturrock and Ralph Milne to frustrate United in the first leg of their UEFA Cup first-round tie at Tannadice. Dodds does manage to beat the Dutch stopper, but Willi van der Kerkhof beats Paul Hegarty to a long ball and fires an away goal past Hamish McAlpine. The 1-1 result leaves the Tangerines facing a tough task in the away leg two weeks later.

WEDNESDAY 16th SEPTEMBER 1981

Prince Rainier and Princess Grace (Grace Kelly) of Monaco are among the spectators who witness an excellent performance and result from United, who beat AS Monaco 5-2 away in the UEFA Cup. Billy Kirkwood opens the scoring with a towering header in the 15th minute, before Paul Sturrock sets Davie Dodds up to make it 2-0 five minutes later. Swedish international Ralf Edström pulls one back for the home side in the second half, before the one-way traffic resumes, with Eamonn Bannon scoring two penalties and Dodds getting his second of the very successful night. A Hamish McAlpine mistake in the last minute gifts Monaco a second consolation goal, but that's not enough to stop *The Glasgow Herald* calling it United's finest hour in Europe, while French daily *Nice Matin* says 'we did not think that AS Monaco could be beaten so emphatically by anyone'. Jim McLean later describes the match as the turning point in United's European campaigns.

WEDNESDAY 17th SEPTEMBER 1986

Paul Sturrock and Kevin Gallacher both have goals ruled out as United dominate the second half of their UEFA Cup first round first leg, away to Lens, with left-back Chris Sulley impressing in the first of just eight matches that he plays for the Tangerines. But United can't find an equaliser to the French side's first-half goal, and the tie is finely poised as the match finishes 1-0 to the home side.

SATURDAY 17th SEPTEMBER 1938

Following Dundee's relegation the previous season, the Dundee derby takes place in the Second Division for the first time, and United win 3-0, at Tannadice. Horace Woolley, playing the first of only three matches for the Tannadice side, scores twice, before the heavens open. *The Courier*'s Don John reports that 'a thousand umbrellas were hoisted and a thousand Dundee hopes crashed as [Dundee goalie Johnny] Lynch conceded a freakish third' when United left-half Andrew Meikleham lobs the ball forward from midfield, Lynch comes to take it but slips and falls on his back, and the ball bounces into the net to seal the home side's victory. Don John says 'the better balanced and more convincing team merited the generous praise of a generous crowd'.

SATURDAY 17th SEPTEMBER 1910

Dundee Hibs earn their first ever victory in the Second Division, coming back after losing a first-minute goal against Abercorn to win 4-1. Centre-forward William Swan, making his debut, scores a hat-trick, with his equaliser coming in just the second minute, but he only plays eight more times for the club, scoring four more goals. James O'Gara – who *The Courier* credits as by far and away the most prominent forward on the field – gets Hibs' fourth goal, late in the game, at the start of a seven-match unbeaten run in the league for the Tannadice men.

WEDNESDAY 17th SEPTEMBER 1980

United have a terrible build-up to their UEFA Cup first leg, away against Śląsk Wrocław in Poland, with travel problems, injuries and an outbreak of flu. Because of the injuries, 32-year-old Walter Smith returns for his first game for over a year, while Davie Dodds – a week before his 22nd birthday – fills in for top scorer Willie Pettigrew, one of the flu victims. Dodds has the ball in the net twice, but both efforts are ruled out for infringements, and the young striker and Eamonn Bannon each have penalty claims turned down, but in spite of the adversity, the Tangerines secure a goalless draw that puts them in the driving seat ahead of the home leg.

SATURDAY 17th SEPTEMBER 1960

Three games into United's first season back in the top flight since 1932, a 3-1 victory over Dundee in front of 20,000 fans at Tannadice puts the Terrors top of the table, above Rangers and Third Lanark on goal average. Tommy Campbell scores two of United's goals and Jimmy Briggs gets the other.

FRIDAY 17th SEPTEMBER 1982

Charlie George strains a calf muscle in training, which rules him out of making his planned United debut against Hibs the following day. The former Arsenal star was signed because of injuries to other strikers and a lack of cover, and ex-Hibs star Ally McLeod is also recruited for the same reason, but both veteran strikers are hampered by injury and neither plays for the Tangerines.

SATURDAY 17th SEPTEMBER 1955

On a bumpy, sodden Firs Park pitch, in high wind and heavy rain, United and East Stirling play out a match that *The Courier* describes as freakish. It rains goals, with Tom McGairy and Johnny Coyle getting two each for the Terrors, and it's 4-4 with just a few minutes left when the home side win a penalty and take a 5-4 lead. But United run straight upfield from kick-off, Coyle is brought down in the box, and Alan Massie fires home from the spot to make it 5-5, with the last kick of United's joint highest-scoring draw ever.

WEDNESDAY 18th SEPTEMBER 1974

Paul Sturrock makes his Dundee United debut, coming on as a substitute for the last half-hour in the European Cup Winners' Cup, as United comfortably beat Romanian side Jiul Petroşani 3-0 at home. Sturrock is incorrectly credited as United's youngest ever European debutant, because when he signed for United he told Jim McLean that he was a year younger than he actually was; McLean isn't happy when Sturrock confesses the truth. *The Glasgow Herald* reports that the scoreline flatters the visitors, with the Tangerines' goals coming from Dave Narey, Jackie Copland and Pat Gardner.

TUESDAY 18th SEPTEMBER 1973

United – who are joint top of the league – visit Bramall Lane to take on Sheffield United – who have four Scottish players in their team – in the Texaco Cup. *The Glasgow Herald* reports that the crowd could not have wished for a more thrilling match, and Hamish McAlpine makes a series of outstanding saves. Unfortunately, at the other end, the Tangerines are too often over-elaborate in front of goal, and the match finishes 0-0.

WEDNESDAY 18th SEPTEMBER 1985

Paul Sturrock gets a hat-trick and Eamonn Bannon scores twice as United win 5-2 away in Europe, against Bohemians in Dublin. The Tangerines play brilliantly and the home side are fortunate not to concede several more goals, with United's fifth goal being the best of the night, as seven players are involved in the build-up before Sturrock fires it into the top corner from 18 yards.

WEDNESDAY 18th SEPTEMBER 1957

Dave Sturrock and Johnny Coyle each score twice – with Coyle also coming close to grabbing at least two more – while Wilson Humphries gets one, as United equal their record high-scoring draw, in an exciting 5-5 tie with Arbroath.

WEDNESDAY 19th SEPTEMBER 1923

The SFA vote on whether to allow Dundee Hibs to change their name to Dundee City, after Dundee said the name change could lead to confusion. Eight members are in favour of allowing the name change, while eight vote against, and the chairman – Celtic's Tom White – is given the casting vote. He says that the club should not be called Dundee City but that other new names would be acceptable, such as Dundee Shamrock or Dundee Wanderers. So the club that came so close to becoming known as Dundee City have to come up with a new alternative.

SATURDAY 19th SEPTEMBER 1925

Early in their first ever season in the top flight, United pull off a shock by beating a highly regarded young Celtic team – who've won all four of their league matches so far in the season, and who go on to win the league – 1-0 at home, in front of 20,000 fans. *The Courier* reports that United's goal, scored late on by Jimmy Howieson, from 30 yards out, is in keeping with the victory – a great one – and that 'the win was really a triumph for the United's defence', who 'held the Celtic line valiantly', and that the Celtic forwards, including the great Jimmy McGrory, 'might as well have pitted their strength against a brick wall'.

SATURDAY 20th SEPTEMBER 1986

Jim McInally makes his debut for United as they beat Hamilton 5-1 away, with the goals coming from Paul Sturrock and doubles from Paul Hegarty and Iain Ferguson. Jim McLean says: 'I know it is unusual for me to say it, but there was a spell in the second half out there when we were magnificent. The pitch was not conducive to good football, but we were in a different class. Jim McInally was the best player on the field.'

TUESDAY 21st SEPTEMBER 1954

Former England international Reggie Smith is appointed as United manager, with the club saying that 'the directors are confident that he is the man to restore the fortunes of the club, and eventually give the club A Division football'. Smith joins from Dundee, where he signed as a player at the end of the Second World War – after being stationed at Leuchars with the RAF – and then became a coach. His reign at Tannadice is marked by gradual improvement, until he leaves early in 1957 to take over at top-flight Falkirk.

SATURDAY 21st SEPTEMBER 1957

The first section of the covered enclosure that will become known as the Shed opens, for a league match against St Johnstone, which United win 2-1. The ground improvements are funded by money raised from the successful Taypools venture, which plays a big part in providing the financial basis for the club's impending growth and success.

SUNDAY 22nd SEPTEMBER 2013

Less than two months after making his debut, 19-year-old Andy Robertson scores his first goal for United, giving the Tangerines a 2-1 lead against Motherwell, as he runs with the ball from his own half and fires home from 20 yards. Unfortunately, Lionel Ainsworth equalises with an equally impressive goal 20 minutes later.

WEDNESDAY 23rd SEPTEMBER 1981

In heavy rain at Tannadice, Graeme Payne, Davie Dodds, Paul Sturrock, John Reilly and Billy Kirkwood all score as United beat Hamilton 5-0 in the second leg of the League Cup quarter-final, to win the tie 9-0 on aggregate. *The Evening Telegraph* says that, in spite of the mismatch, it's a great night of football, full of fine moves and goalmouth thrills, and that Payne's one-twos with Sturrock and Dave Narey 'were so cheeky they drew delighted laughter first, then applause'. Jim McLean says, 'I was pleased to see so many fans turn out in such dreadful weather. It gave me a kick to note we had twice as many spectators at our game as Rangers had at Ibrox [against Brechin].' The Tangerines will face a sterner test in the semi-final, against Aberdeen.

TUESDAY 23rd SEPTEMBER 1975

At the age of 19, Dave Narey scores both goals as United beat Icelandic side Keflavík 2-0, away, in the UEFA Cup. Andy Gray, making his last appearance for United before he's transferred to Wolves, sets up Narey's first goal.

SATURDAY 24th SEPTEMBER 1966

United visit Ayr in the league, and the match is goalless at half-time, before Jerry Kerr moves Ian Mitchell to centre-forward, and the floodgates open in the second half. Mitchell, Finn Døssing and Örjan Persson each score twice as the Terrors win 7-0. Kerr says, 'That should give us all the confidence we need. And we do need it, with Rangers coming here on Saturday.' Unfortunately United lose narrowly in that game with the men from Ibrox.

WEDNESDAY 25th SEPTEMBER 1996

John Souttar is born on this day in Aberdeen. Just 16 years and 99 days later, he becomes United's youngest ever player, when he partners Jon Daly in the centre of defence, in a 2-2 draw away to Aberdeen. It's the first of 73 United appearances for the talented young defender, who features regularly for Scotland under-17s, under-19s and under-21s during his time at Tannadice. Souttar remains United's youngest player until 2019.

SATURDAY 26th SEPTEMBER 1998

Billy Dodds scores a hat-trick on his first start for United, a 3-1 victory away to St Johnstone. His first is an impressive looping header from the edge of the box, his second comes from a fiercely struck penalty after Stuart McCluskey pulls down Kjell Olofsson, and for his third he plays a one-two with Gary McSwegan, chips Alan Main, runs round him and volleys his own pass into the net. Manager Paul Sturrock is proud of getting Dodds for a good price. Dons boss Alex Miller had phoned him to enquire about Robbie Winters' availability, and Sturrock replied by asking about the possibility of a swap deal for Dodds, who he rated higher than Winters. Sturrock is surprised when, as well as agreeing, Miller offers him £200,000 on top, but Sturrock still manages to negotiate the extra money up to £600,000 for United.

WEDNESDAY 26th SEPTEMBER 1984

United beat Hearts 2-1, away, in a very physical League Cup semi-final first leg. Eight players are booked, and Dave Narey and Hearts' Dave Bowman are both sent off when Narey uses his fists to react to a Bowman foul. Hamish McAlpine – making his first appearance of the season – has to pick the ball out of the net in the first minute after John Robertson opens the scoring with a free kick from 30 yards. In a match that he describes as 'rough, rugged and wild', *The Glasgow Herald*'s Ian Paul says 'United were the better team, particularly in the second half, when they managed to reduce the pace to hectic', and two second-half John Clark headers set the Tangerines up nicely for the home leg.

TUESDAY 27th SEPTEMBER 1977

Defending a 1-0 lead from the home leg, United play Copenhagen – whose team includes Finn Laudrup; Michael and Brian's dad – away in the UEFA Cup. Jim McLean promises that the Terrors will attack, and they have several chances to grab an away goal in the first half, but Danish keeper Ole Qvist makes a string of impressive saves, and in the second half it all goes wrong, as Torsten Andersen grabs a hat-trick to knock United out.

WEDNESDAY 28th SEPTEMBER 1983

Jim McLean predicts that all 11 Hamrun Spartans players will play in their own half – and sometimes all 'encamped' in their own penalty area – in the second leg of their European Cup tie, as they just aim to keep the scoreline fairly respectable, and he's not wrong. Defending with so many men can have its disadvantages though, and Ralph Milne and Billy Kirkwood both score from deflected shots in the first half, while, between those goals, goalkeeper Charles Brincat achieves the ironic distinction of being booked for time wasting when his side are 4-0 down on aggregate. Less than a minute after the break, Ralph Milne – after running out of play – nips back onto the pitch to knock home a rebound, and make it 3-0, without being flagged offside. 'By that time,' says *The Glasgow Herald*, 'nobody was caring' about details like offside, and United's first ever European Cup tie ends in a 6-0 aggregate victory.

TUESDAY 28th SEPTEMBER 1993

Trailing 2-0 from the away leg of their UEFA Cup first-round tie, United beat Brøndby 2-0 over the 90 minutes at Tannadice, to take the tie to extra time. The goals come in the second half, through a low Billy McKinlay shot from the edge of the box and – 11 minutes from the end – from Scott Crabbe, after he plays a swift one-two with Paddy Connolly. But, just 20 seconds into extra time, the Tangerines have it all to do again, as Jesper Kristensen scores an away goal. John Clark equalises in the last minute of extra time, but United go out on away goals.

WEDNESDAY 29th SEPTEMBER 1982

Dutch first division leaders PSV lose at home in European competition for just the second time in 27 years, as United come to Eindhoven and beat them 2-0. *The Glasgow Herald* says that United 'excelled themselves', with Paul Sturrock and Eamonn Bannon combining to set up Billy Kirkwood, who volleys home the opening goal after just five minutes, and Paul Hegarty making it two 25 minutes later, after a clever Milne dummy. Bannon has the ball in the net too although it's ruled out for offside. It doesn't matter though, as the Terrors win 3-1 on aggregate, to set up a second-round tie with Viking Stavanger.

WEDNESDAY 30th SEPTEMBER 1964

Playing in the League Cup semi-final, against Rangers, United come within four minutes of earning their place in the final. They defend well and put together some attractive moves further forward but just have one goal – a first-half header from Doug Moran, who's only at Tannadice for a few months – to show for it. But in the last ten minutes Rangers earn a series of corners, they send everyone forward, and, with just a few minutes left to play, Jim Forrest equalises. In extra time, United fire in four shots, but Rangers goalie Billy Ritchie saves them all well, and Forrest scores his second, when Doug Smith has a chance to clear the ball, but Forrest shouts 'leave it Doug', fooling the United defender into thinking that one of his own team-mates has it under control and allowing the cheeky Ranger to grab the winner.

TUESDAY 30th SEPTEMBER 1975

United stretch their unbeaten record at home in Europe to 13 games as they comfortably beat Keflavík 4-0 in the second leg of their UEFA Cup tie, at a misty Tannadice, with Henry Hall scoring twice, either side of goals from Paul Hegarty and Paul Sturrock. Another Icelandic side, Valur, are among the crowd, ahead of their Cup Winners' Cup tie against Celtic the next day.

WEDNESDAY 30th SEPTEMBER 1981

Clearly bearing no ill will following their side's heavy defeat at home, Prince Rainier and Princess Grace of Monaco are in the Tannadice crowd as Monaco visit Tayside for the second leg of their UEFA Cup tie. And the royal couple see their side make a good effort of overcoming the Tangerines' 5-2 lead from the first leg. In his programme notes, Jim McLean says he's looking for no slackness and an early goal to settle the tie. But that's not what he gets. United have early chances, but the visitors score early in the second half and again ten minutes later, as United look nervous. But, 15 minutes from the end, McLean brings on Ralph Milne, who scores the goal that puts the result beyond any doubt, with United going through 6-4 on aggregate.

DUNDEE UNITED

ON THIS DAY

OCTOBER

WEDNESDAY 1st OCTOBER 1969

Trailing 2-1 from the first leg of their Fairs Cup tie, United play well away to Newcastle, with Alex Reid, who's particularly impressive, cracking a shot against the post in the first half, while the Terrors' defence keep the Magpies' forwards under control. But the goals don't come for the men from Tannadice, and Keith Dyson grabs a goal for the home side at the death. *The Glasgow Herald* describes the result as a travesty of justice.

SATURDAY 1st OCTOBER 1921

Back in Division Two after spending a season in the Central League, Dundee Hibs beat Clackmannan 7-1, with five of their goals coming in the second half. *The Courier* reports that all of Hibs' goals are 'the outcome of clever efforts', with Lowingham Braidford and Horace Williams getting two each and Dan Gibson, Willie Hogg and Tom Bannister scoring one apiece. Hibs finish the season second from bottom, above Clackmannan, and play in the Scottish Alliance in the next season.

WEDNESDAY 1st OCTOBER 1986

Ralph Milne scores his 15th goal in Europe as United overcome a tricky 1-0 first-leg deficit to beat Lens 2-0 at home, and win their tie on aggregate, on a nervous night when Dave Narey and Iain Ferguson are both unavailable. Lens are set up to defend, and their goalie Gaetan Huard makes some great saves to keep the game goalless until after half-time. But United hold their nerve and Milne breaks the deadlock ten minutes into the second half, firing low into the net from near the penalty spot after Paul Sturrock sets him up. Five minutes later Milne turns provider for Tommy Coyne to double the advantage and put United in the pot for the second round.

WEDNESDAY 1st OCTOBER 1980

United beat Śląsk Wrocław 7-2 at home in the UEFA Cup. Davie Dodds and Willie Pettigrew score two each, with the others coming from Derek Stark, Paul Hegarty and a Graeme Payne penalty. *The Glasgow Herald* says that Śląsk – an army-sponsored team – will be getting a court martial 'on their return east of the Iron Curtain.'

TUESDAY 2nd OCTOBER 1979

Hamish McAlpine returns to the side for the second leg of United's UEFA Cup tie with Anderlecht, in Belgium, after Peter Bonetti conceded four goals to Morton at the weekend. After the first leg finished goalless, United start well in Brussels but it's the home side who break the deadlock halfway through the first half, and McAlpine has to pull off some great saves to keep the Tangerines in it, before, ten minutes from the end, Paul Sturrock makes a great run and finds Frank Kopel, who smashes the ball into the top corner from 20 yards, sending the small group of Arabs in the 30,000 crowd wild, as United go through on away goals. Bonetti doesn't play for United again, with McAlpine now established back in the side.

WEDNESDAY 2nd OCTOBER 1974

Following a difficult journey through mountains to the small mining town of Petroşani in Transylvania in Romania, United take to the field in the second leg of their European Cup Winners' Cup tie against Jiul Petroşani. Local miners are given the day off so that they can watch the match, and the Tangerines' three-goal lead from the home leg is badly threatened as the Romanians score twice in the first half, in front of a 15,000 capacity crowd. Jim McLean brings on Tommy Traynor in the second half, which seems to settle United nerves as they see out the aggregate win to qualify for the second round.

WEDNESDAY 3rd OCTOBER 1984

Trailing 1-0 from the away leg, United leave it until the second half at home to overcome AIK Stockholm in the UEFA Cup. The visitors come close to getting an away goal twice in the first half: in the first minute when Tommy Johansson misses from six yards, and then when Tommy Andersson forces Hamish McAlpine into a great save from 25 yards. But the Tangerines are vastly improved in the second half. One minute after the restart, Paul Sturrock knocks the ball home from a rebound after Davie Dodds' shot is saved, and then Ralph Milne scores twice in a four-minute spell, capitalising on two defensive mistakes, to give United a victory that's much more comfortable than it initially seemed it would be.

WEDNESDAY 3rd OCTOBER 1973

Dundee United make light work of Sheffield United at home in the second leg of their Texaco Cup tie, winning 2-0 on the night and on aggregate, through two Jim Henry goals, as the frustrated Blades have four men booked.

WEDNESDAY 4th OCTOBER 1995

Andy McLaren sets up all four goals as United thump Dunfermline in the Challenge Cup semi-final. Christian Dailly opens the scoring after three minutes, Grant Johnson gets one and Robbie Winters scores twice, before being sent off for arguing with a linesman.

SATURDAY 5th OCTOBER 1963

United beat Airdrie 9-1. Tommy Millar, Jim Irvine, Dennis Gillespie and Ian Mitchell each get doubles, before Jimmy Briggs adds the ninth. The Terrors' Stewart Fraser also gets on the scoresheet, but at the wrong end, as he briefly brings the Diamonds level, early on.

SATURDAY 5th OCTOBER 1991

Argentina international Victor Ferreyra scores twice in his second game for United, a 4-0 win over Falkirk. Although Ferreyra – for whom United paid £350,000 – is clearly talented and is initially popular with the fans, it's all downhill from here, with a modest goalscoring return and unsavoury outbreaks of anger in matches against Rangers and Dundee. In 1993, he moves to Japan.

FRIDAY 6th OCTOBER 1995

Gary McSwegan signs for United, for £350,000, from Notts County. He scores 43 goals in his first three seasons at Tannadice, even though many of his appearances come as a substitute.

MONDAY 7th OCTOBER 2002

Paul Hegarty becomes United caretaker manager, as the club court Falkirk manager Ian McCall as permanent boss. United chairman Eddie Thompson has a meeting with McCall's agent the next day, but McCall announces that he's staying at Brockville. In November, Hegarty is given the job for the rest of the season, but in February, with United bottom of the league, he's sacked, and replaced by... Ian McCall.

WEDNESDAY 8th OCTOBER 1969

United's alter egos become their opponents, as Dallas Tornado – who are now a club in their own right and don't need United to represent them any more – visit Tannadice for a friendly, in what *The Evening Telegraph* describes as 'far from Texas-like weather'. The match is a good contest, with the multi-national Tornado team taking the lead through Dutchman Hank Liotart before Dennis Gillespie equalises from the penalty spot and Ian Scott gives the Terrors the lead. Serbian midfielder Ilija Mitić equalises before Kenny Cameron seals a 3-2 win for United. The Tornado last until 1981, longer than any of the 11 other American clubs that started at the same time.

SATURDAY 9th OCTOBER 1943

Albert Juliussen scores four as United beat Falkirk 7-1, taking his record for the season so far to 15 goals from seven games. In spite of the resounding scoreline, *The Evening Telegraph* credits Falkirk with a 'snappy display'. United's other goalscorers are Willie Wann, who gets one, and George Thomson, who knocks two penalties home.

WEDNESDAY 9th OCTOBER 1985

Goalie Hamish McAlpine makes his 625th – and last – appearance for United, at the age of 37, in the League Cup semi-final second leg at Pittodrie. McAlpine, who'd been named the Scottish Football Writers' Player of the Year at the end of the previous season, sustains a serious leg injury in the first half, but soldiers on with a bandage on his knee until the 73rd minute, when he's substituted and Paul Hegarty goes in goal.

TUESDAY 10th OCTOBER 2006

David Goodwillie scores the only goal of the game as Scotland under-19s beat Germany under-19s – including Mesut Özil – and top their UEFA Championship qualifying group. Goodwillie's goal comes halfway through the first half, when he collects the ball with his back to goal, on the edge of the penalty area, turns, beats two defenders and shoots into the bottom corner. Two minutes later, the United teenager – who also scored a hat-trick against Bosnia five days earlier – hits the post, and in the second half he hits the side netting from a tight angle.

WEDNESDAY 10th OCTOBER 1984

Hearts defender Walter Kidd is booked after just 12 seconds at Tannadice, in the second leg of a League Cup semi-final that United win comfortably. Two players had been sent off in a combustible first leg, but on this night referee Brian McGinlay keeps a lid on things, and it's the police who restore order, making several arrests when Hearts fans spill onto the pitch and the game has to stop for a minute. In the first half, man of the match Eamonn Bannon gives the Terrors the lead on the night with a clever free kick. After the break, Paul Sturrock flicks a Bannon pass to Davie Dodds to score United's second, and Bannon is involved yet again as Billy Kirkwood makes it three on the night. Although Donald Park gets a late consolation goal for the Jam Tarts, the Tangerines march on to the final against Rangers, thanks to a 5-2 aggregate win.

MONDAY 11th OCTOBER 1976

Rangers' John Greig and Celtic's Ronnie Glavin both score for United as they draw 7-7 with Dundee. The unusual match with the remarkable scoreline is a testimonial for United winger Iain McDonald, who has had to retire at the age of 23 because of injury. As well as the two guests from Glasgow, Graeme Payne and Tom McAdam each grab a goal for the Tangerines, while Paul Hegarty gets a double and Bobby Ford scores an own goal. Teenager Gordon Strachan and Aberdeen's Jocky Scott each get hat-tricks for the Dark Blues, whose side includes United's Doug Houston.

SATURDAY 12th OCTOBER 1974

Tommy Traynor scores a hat-trick as United outclass Hearts, beating the Edinburgh side 5-0. Doug Houston opens the scoring in the first minute, and Andy Gray gets the Terrors' other goal. Dave McLaren, an Auchterarder-born football manager who's working in Australia but back visiting Dundee, gives his verdict on Gray's value, saying, 'I'd give my grandstand to take a player like that back with me.' And following the match, there's lots of speculation linking Jim McLean with the vacant manager's position at Tynecastle, but of course he stays at Tannadice. McLean later confirms that he was twice offered the Hearts job.

Eamonn Bannon was a key player in the glory years, creating and scoring many goals

TUESDAY 13th OCTOBER 1936

Jimmy Brownlie resigns from his second spell as Dundee United manager, as the club experiences financial difficulties and director George Greig takes over responsibility for team affairs. Two years later, Brownlie returns for a third and final spell as manager.

SATURDAY 13th OCTOBER 2018

Robbie Neilson's first game in charge of United ends in victory, 2-1 away against Partick Thistle. Pavol Šafranko and Fraser Aird get the goals for the Terrors, and it's only former United keeper Cammy Bell who keeps the scoreline respectable for the home side, with good saves from Callum Booth, Frederic Frans and Šafranko, while Paul McMullan hits a post and Šafranko has another effort ruled out. Neilson says, 'The players and the fans were brilliant.'

TUESDAY 13th OCTOBER 1964

With United struggling for results, Jerry Kerr, on the look-out for new players, goes to Dunfermline's Fairs Cup tie against Swedish side Örgryte, where he's particularly impressed by two of the visitors' players, half-back Lennart Wing, and winger Örjan Persson. They will both soon become very familiar to United fans.

WEDNESDAY 14th OCTOBER 2015

Mixu Paatelainen is appointed as manager, with United at the bottom of the league. The big Finn says, 'It feels wonderful. Obviously this club is special to me – it was my first club abroad as a player. Fond memories.' Chairman Stephen Thompson says: 'It's exciting times, it's a fresh start for the club.' Unfortunately the results early in Paatelainen's reign aren't good, and although they improve in the new year, it's not enough to save the club from relegation, and Paatelainen is sacked the day after the club's fate is confirmed.

WEDNESDAY 15th OCTOBER 1997

United beat Aberdeen 3-1 in the League Cup semi-final. Robbie Winters scores twice, and 18-year-old Craig Easton gets his first ever United goal, which he celebrates in the style of Fabrizio Ravanelli. 'That was a bit embarrassing,' he says. 'It was spur of the moment and I don't know what came over me.'

SATURDAY 16th OCTOBER 1965

Finn Døssing opens the scoring after just 14 seconds against Hamilton, in a home match that United win 7-0, with two goals from Frannie Munro, two penalties from Lennart Wing, a solitary Benny Rooney strike and a second goal for Døssing. After the match an Accies fan sets fire to his red and white scarf, while the result takes United's goal tally to 28 in their first seven league games of the season, and puts them joint top of the Premier Division with Rangers.

SATURDAY 16th OCTOBER 1982

Davie Dodds gets a hat-trick but two-goal Dave Narey steals the show, as devastating United destroy Morton 6-0 at Tannadice, with four of the goals coming in a six-minute spell in the first half. Billy Kirkwood gets the Terrors' other goal, and Morton boss Benny Rooney says, 'It is suicide to stand and admire United when they are in that kind of form.' Meanwhile, Jim McLean emphasises that the result was the reward for a great team performance, but also says: 'That Narey display simply had to be seen to be believed. For long enough I have listened with disbelief at stories from south of the border concerning this player being valued at £1 million plus. Well, if there is such a thing as a footballer worth that kind of money, then for me it has got to be Dave Narey.' The valuation comes just three and a half years after the first ever million-pound transfer.

TUESDAY 17th OCTOBER 1989

Paul Hegarty's 707th and final United appearance isn't a happy one, as he's substituted after 50 minutes of a 4-0 defeat away to Royal Antwerp in the second round of the UEFA Cup. Jim McLean says: 'I would not expect an amateur team to lose goals the way we did. All four goals were suicidal.' But McLean's selection of a central defensive partnership of Hegarty and Dave Narey – who have contributed so much to United's success for so many years, but who now have a combined age of 68 – contributes significantly to the defeat against a Belgian team that attacks swiftly, and that scores three goals in one ten-minute spell in the first half.

WEDNESDAY 17th OCTOBER 1923

Dundee Hibs and Dundee finally reach agreement on Dundee Hibs' name change. Following an SFA meeting in Glasgow, representatives of both clubs meet and agree on the name change to Dundee United, rather than the Dundee City name that Hibs had preferred and that Dundee objected to.

SATURDAY 18th OCTOBER 1924

United beat Arthurlie 4-1 at Tannadice, to stretch their unbeaten run to ten games at the start of the Division Two season. All five goals come in one 30-minute period in the second half. Right-winger Tommy Simpson opens the scoring with a deflected shot, before Bobby Bauld scores a penalty then gets another as he converts a great Simpson cross. And, after the visitors pull one back, Sandy Gilmour completes the scoring, with another deflected shot, as United top the table. With a General Election coming up 11 days later, political candidates Edwin Scrymgeour, Frederick William Wallace and Edmund Dene Morel are at the match, but there's no success from the right wing in the election, as Scrymgeour (Scottish Prohibition Party) and Morel (Labour) are both elected.

WEDNESDAY 19th OCTOBER 1983

United play with impressive composure, confidence and discipline as they draw 0-0 away against Standard Liege in the first leg of a European Cup second-round tie that Jim McLean later describes as – across both matches – the club's most perfect performances in Europe. Belgian goalie Michel Preud'homme has to make a series of good saves, with United so dominant that the Belgian fans jeer and whistle their players at half-time and then boo them at the end.

SATURDAY 20th OCTOBER 1923

Dundee Hibs win their last ever game before they change their name, beating top-of-the-table King's Park 3-2 away, in what *The Evening Telegraph* calls Hibs' best performance of the season so far, in a match that's 'remarkable for its keenness, cleanness, pace and excitement'. In an exciting ten-minute first-half period, each team scores twice, and Sandy Gilmour – playing on the left wing for the first time – scores the only goal after that, as Dundee Hibs sign off with an impressive victory.

TUESDAY 20th OCTOBER 1981

In the first leg of their UEFA Cup second round tie, in Germany, United play fantastically for the first 70 minutes against Borussia Mönchengladbach. Paul Hegarty and Dave Narey defend excellently, while Ralph Milne and Eamonn Bannon each come close to getting an away goal, with Nottingham Forest assistant manager Peter Taylor an interested spectator in the stands. But the Tangerines lose to two late goals – the second of which comes just three minutes from the end – leaving themselves with it all to do at Tannadice. But Jim McLean, who describes the result as a travesty, says that there's no way that the tie is finished.

SATURDAY 20th OCTOBER 1945

Willie MacFadyen's reign as United manager gets off to a brilliant start as United beat Stenhousemuir 7-0 in his first game in charge, with four of the goals coming in the last 11 minutes. United's success comes in spite of having new faces and a forced change in the team. When Tommy Dunsmore misses a train, David Jack has to step in at short notice, while inside-left Ronald Aitken – a trialist from Croy Celtic, who turns down a contract offer from United after the game – scores a hat-trick in his only game for the club, and winger Leslie Young – stationed locally with the RAF – and centre-forward Emilio Pacione – playing his first senior game after signing from Lochee Harp – both also score on their debuts, with Pacione getting two. Charlie Ferguson is the relative veteran among the goalscorers, playing in his sixth match for United.

WEDNESDAY 21st OCTOBER 1970

Goalie Hamish McAlpine makes his second ever appearance for Dundee United when he comes on as a substitute for injured Don Mackay, away to Sparta Prague in the first leg of their Fairs Cup second-round tie. The Terrors play well for the first hour, attacking with speed. Tommy Traynor equalises after the home side's Václav Vrána opens the scoring, but Sparta retake the lead with 20 minutes to go, through Josef Jurkanin, Andy Rolland is sent off ten minutes later for kicking the ball away at a free kick, and, on the stroke of full time, Jurkanin gets his second, making the final score 3-1 to the Czechs.

WEDNESDAY 22nd OCTOBER 1986

After scoring four goals in four UEFA Cup games in the previous season, Ian Redford scores twice in one first leg match as United leave it late to beat Universitatea Craiova 3-0 on a bitterly cold night at Tannadice. The Romanians' goalie makes some good saves, from Redford and Dave Bowman, and the home fans are patient as they wait for the first goal, which comes ten minutes into the second half, when a John Clark header from a Ralph Milne corner sets Redford up to open the scoring. It remains 1-0 until the 80th minute, when Clark heads home from a Bowman corner, and Redford gets the third two minutes from time, knocking home the rebound from a Maurice Malpas shot. With two of the goals coming so late, *The Glasgow Herald* reports that 'The Romanians left the pitch scratching their heads in bewilderment. They were merely the latest victims of United's experience, expertise and patient determination in the European battlefront.'

SATURDAY 23rd OCTOBER 1948

United and Arbroath share ten goals in a thrilling draw at Tannadice. United lead 3-2 at half-time, through Frank Quinn, Jimmy Dickson and Peter McKay, but the Red Lichties score twice more to get their noses in front midway through the tempestuous second half, before goals from George Cruickshank and George Grant put the home side back on top. But the visitors' Willie Ross equalises at full time. Arbroath's former manager, Bob McGlashan, says: 'It was one of the hardest derbies I can remember. The result was a good one, although it was galling for United to lose a point with the last kick of the game.'

SATURDAY 23rd OCTOBER 1982

United go 21 consecutive games unbeaten, as they beat Motherwell 2-0, but Jim McLean's unimpressed, saying: 'Several performances made me unhappy. Some of my players looked jaded and I was definitely disappointed.' With Paul Sturrock and Eamonn Bannon out injured, the Tangerines can't score until the last minute, when Dave Narey blasts home a 25-yard shot from the same mould as his goal against Brazil four months earlier, and, almost immediately after that, Ralph Milne runs to the byline and cuts the ball back for Billy Kirkwood to make it two.

WEDNESDAY 23rd OCTOBER 1985

Vardar Skopje, from Macedonia in Yugoslavia, come to Tannadice for a first leg match in the UEFA Cup second round, apparently with just one thing on their minds: preventing United from scoring, by any means necessary. Paul Sturrock in particular is repeatedly fouled, and East German referee Bernd Stumpf has to show the visitors the yellow card five times and the red twice, and also order one of their coaches to leave the dug-out. Jim McLean says their tactics are a shame particularly because they have some talented players, and adds that he's never been prouder of Sturrock, who displays impressive professionalism and bravery in the face of provocation. And, in spite of Vardar's tactics, Ian Redford and Richard Gough both score, giving United a reasonably healthy advantage ahead of the away leg.

WEDNESDAY 24th OCTOBER 1984

A great performance away from home by United in the UEFA Cup second round first leg, as they beat Linz ASK 2-1 in Austria. Dave Narey, Paul Sturrock and Ralph Milne combine to set up Billy Kirkwood to open the scoring after 15 minutes, before Max Hagmayr equalises. And in the last minute, Sturrock is fouled in the box, the Romanian referee points to the spot, and Eamonn Bannon fires home another away goal. Jim McLean – who always prefers playing away from home first in Europe – says: 'I am delighted with the team's performance. It was one of the best ever away from home in Europe. We created more chances than we took, and all credit to the players, who played their hearts out tonight. Paul Sturrock tore the heart out of the Austrian defence, but I don't really want to single out any one player. It was a great team effort.'

WEDNESDAY 24th OCTOBER 1973

For the second consecutive season, United face Leicester City in the Texaco Cup – this time in the quarter-final – and for the second time in a row they draw the first leg, at Filbert Street, 1-1. Frank Worthington opens the scoring for the Foxes from the penalty spot early in the second half, before a deflected Frank Kopel shot beats young Peter Shilton, to give the Tangerines a good chance of reaching the semi-final.

TUESDAY 25th OCTOBER 1966

United play in European competition for the first time, and are thrown in at the deep end in the Fairs Cup, away against the holders, Barcelona. The Terrors rise to the challenge with style, with Billy Hainey scoring the club's first goal in Europe – repeating a trick that he had also performed for Partick Thistle – after just 13 minutes. In the second half, Hainey wins a penalty, which Finn Seemann scores, and Barcelona can only pull one back, ten minutes from the end. United's 2-1 victory – which *The Daily Record* says will ring around Europe – makes them the first Scottish team to win in Spain.

SATURDAY 26th OCTOBER 1996

Swedish striker Kjell Olofsson and Norwegian midfielder Erik Pedersen – who's playing as a trialist – both make their United debuts, in a 1-0 victory over Hearts, early in Tommy McLean's time in charge at Tannadice, as the new manager brings in Scandinavian recruits as part of his plan to turn around the club's bad start to the season. Olofsson, who signed for the Tangerines just before the Hearts game, says: 'Scottish football is very different from Norway and Sweden – but I was quite happy with today. As I get used to the new team, and they get used to me, I hope I will do better.' It doesn't take the popular Swede long to fulfil his potential at Tannadice, and he's top scorer in the first two of his three seasons with the Tangerines.

SATURDAY 27th OCTOBER 1934

Bobby Yorke, Bobby Gardiner, Jimmy Smith and Alec King each score twice, as United thump Brechin 8-0, away, and *The Evening Telegraph* says that George Ross would have got two too, if he had 'possessed a shooting boot worthy of the name'. The result leaves United six points off the top of Division Two.

SATURDAY 27th OCTOBER 1923

Life as Dundee United doesn't start well in the club's first game following their name change, away against Dumbarton. The home side take the lead eight minutes before half-time, and it's almost exclusively one-way traffic after that, as United end up losing 3-0.

SATURDAY 27th OCTOBER 1962

In the programme notes ahead of their Division One home match against Raith Rovers, United state that they plan to strengthen their attack, but then demonstrate that they maybe don't need to, as they win 8-1. *The Evening Telegraph* says that nearly every goal is the result of first-class play, as Dennis Gillespie gets a hat-trick, Wattie Carlyle grabs two, and Tommy Neilson, Jim Irvine and 16-year-old Ian Mitchell score one each. It's the first of Mitchell's 113 goals for United. United come close to repeating the high-scoring trick in the return fixture in Kirkcaldy later in the season, when they win 7-2.

SUNDAY 28th OCTOBER 1984

United lose the League Cup Final to Rangers in torrential rain at Hampden. Ralph Milne has to be substituted after just 11 minutes in a disappointing match played in difficult conditions. Both sides have chances but future United striker Iain Ferguson scores the only goal of the game, for Rangers, just before half-time. United have a penalty appeal turned down when Dave McPherson seems to hold Paul Sturrock, and Jim McLean says, 'I have always said that you get out of a game what you put in but I honestly believe that we didn't get what we deserve. At the end of the day it just wasn't for us.'

WEDNESDAY 28th OCTOBER 1981

United go into the League Cup semi-final away leg trailing 1-0 against Aberdeen, who are unbeaten in 13 matches. But Paul Sturrock – who's just back from three weeks out injured – levels the tie on aggregate after just seven minutes, as he picks up a loose ball on the edge of the area, shrugs off the attention of several defenders and sends the ball looping over Jim Leighton into the net. Half an hour later, Leighton fumbles a troublesome Eamonn Bannon cross, and Ralph Milne thumps the ball into the net. And Sturrock puts the tie beyond doubt in the last ten minutes, racing onto a long Billy Kirkwood chip and blasting the ball past Leighton, to send the Tangerines into the final for the third consecutive season, prompting Jim McLean to suggest that the SFA might consider moving Hampden 'a few miles nearer to the east coast'.

WEDNESDAY 29th OCTOBER 2014

United beat Hibs 7-6 on penalties after drawing 3-3 in the League Cup quarter-final at Easter Road. In the first 20 minutes of a dramatic match, United take the lead through Chris Erskine, lose the lead, and then get it back again, through Aiden Connolly. In the second half, Hibs – who are unbeaten in six matches – equalise again, before Ryan Dow makes it 3-2 to the Tangerines, but the home side draw level yet again and the tie goes to penalties. Both teams score their first six, before United's John Rankin misses, but then Radoslaw Cierzniak saves from Matthew Kennedy and – after Conor Townsend scores – pulls off an even better save from David Gray, to send the Terrors into the semi-final, against Aberdeen.

TUESDAY 30th OCTOBER 1979

Using some of the money raised through Ray Stewart's £400,000 transfer to West Ham, United sign midfielder Eamonn Bannon from Chelsea, for a Scottish club record fee of £165,000. Bannon – one of the few non-home-grown players in Jim McLean's United squad – goes straight into the team the next day for a League Cup tie with Raith Rovers, the first of 440 appearances for the Tangerines, during which he scores over 100 goals, becoming one of the top players in United's most successful era, and earning regular appearances for Scotland, including at the 1986 World Cup.

SATURDAY 31st OCTOBER 1987

A disappointing 3-2 defeat to St Mirren has a generously proportioned silver lining as 20-year-old Mixu Paatelainen makes his United debut, sets up the opening goal for Iain Ferguson and scores the Tangerines' second, at the start of a five-year and 47-goal Tannadice career.

TUESDAY 31st OCTOBER 1989

United – eventually – salvage some pride in their home leg against Royal Antwerp, who beat them 4-0 in the first leg. Before the match, Jim McLean praises Antwerp's forwards but says that United must take risks, and in the first half the Belgians add two away goals to their commanding lead. But after that Mixu Paatelainen, Michael O'Neill and John Clark all score, to make the scoreline on the night – although not on aggregate – respectable.

DUNDEE UNITED

ON THIS DAY

NOVEMBER

SATURDAY 1st NOVEMBER 2014

A 3-0 defeat of St Mirren puts United top of the Premiership, with Paul Paton, Nadir Çiftçi and Charlie Telfer – who's making his first start for the Tangerines, after three cameo appearances as a substitute in August – getting the goals.

WEDNESDAY 2nd NOVEMBER 1983

In possibly their greatest ever European performance, United beat Standard Liege 4-0 at home in the second leg of their European Cup second-round tie. Ralph Milne is particularly impressive, scoring twice, with a diving header and a chip, and being involved in the other two, scored by Paul Hegarty and Davie Dodds, as United – described as 'almost flawless' by *The Glasgow Herald* – march into the last eight of the world's greatest club competition, at the first time of asking. Jim McLean gives particular praise to Ralph Milne, with whom he doesn't always see eye-to-eye, and confesses to treating himself 'to a wee smile'.

TUESDAY 3rd NOVEMBER 1981

In another great performance in Europe, United beat Borussia Mönchengladbach 5-0 at home and 5-2 on aggregate in the UEFA Cup second round. The Tangerines have several other good chances to score more, but the convincing scoreline is sealed by strikes from Ralph Milne, Billy Kirkwood, Paul Sturrock, Paul Hegarty and Eamonn Bannon, who runs 45 yards, beating several defenders, and slips the ball past the German goalie, Wolfgang Kleff. Jim McLean says, 'I thought our lads were just marvellous. They did Scotland proud. People talk about West German football, Dutch football and all the rest but I think we showed tonight that Scotland aren't bad either.' Borussia coach Jupp Heynckes says, 'United were a wonderful team and we cannot possibly complain. The scoreline was quite correct.'

SATURDAY 3rd NOVEMBER 1979

Eamonn Bannon scores his first goal for United, four days after signing for the club, in a 3-0 defeat of Aberdeen at Pittodrie. The Terrors' other goals come in the first 15 minutes, from Willie Pettigrew and Iain Phillip, and thousands of Aberdeen fans leave before the final whistle, possibly including *The Evening Express*'s Andy Melvin, who wrongly reports that the match finishes 2-0.

WEDNESDAY 4th NOVEMBER 1970

United narrowly fail to overcome Sparta Prague on aggregate in the Fairs Cup second round, as they dominate their second-leg match on a marshy Tannadice pitch but only score once, and lose 3-2 on aggregate. *The Glasgow Herald* reports that the Terrors 'laid siege to the Sparta Prague goal for 80 of the 90 minutes'. Alan Gordon scores after just 17 minutes, finishing a move that he started, but although United have numerous chances, the Sparta goalie and a 'solid wall of defenders' keep them out.

SUNDAY 5th NOVEMBER 1995

Less than a year and a half after beating Rangers in the Scottish Cup Final at Hampden, United play in another cup final, but this time it's the Challenge Cup, at McDiarmid Park, against a Stenhousemuir side that beat Dundee 3-0 at Dens Park in the quarter-final, and that includes 37-year-old Eamonn Bannon. United have reached the final without conceding a goal, and play 90 minutes, plus extra time, without conceding but also without scoring, as the Warriors defend well and the match goes to penalties, which – on a disappointing day – United lose 5-4.

WEDNESDAY 5th NOVEMBER 1975

Trailing 2-1 from the home leg, United get an impressive 1-1 draw away against Porto in the UEFA Cup, but go out on aggregate. Young Paul Hegarty opens the scoring in the second half in Portugal, but Seninho scores for the home side just five minutes later. It all gets a bit bad-tempered after that, and George Fleming is sent off in the last minute, when he retaliates to a foul.

SUNDAY 5th NOVEMBER 2006

Craig Levein gets off to a great start in his first match as United manager, beating Rangers 2-1 at home. The men from Ibrox open the scoring early in the second half, but Garry Kenneth heads home from a Barry Robson corner 15 minutes from the end and, five minutes after that, Lee Mair also scores with a header, from a Craig Conway cross, to lift the Tangerines off the foot of the table, and send the home crowd – including Lorraine Kelly – wild.

WEDNESDAY 5th NOVEMBER 1986

With Paul Hegarty and Dave Narey out injured, 23-year-old Maurice Malpas captains a young United side in their UEFA Cup second leg match against Universitatea Craiova in Romania. Forty thousand fans squeeze into the Stadionul Central, with others watching from the roofs of neighbouring buildings. Before kick-off, the scoreboard cheekily flashes up the 4-0 scoreline that would send the home side into the third round, but they only score once, and United win 3-1 on aggregate. A proud Jim McLean has particular praise for goalie Billy Thomson, saying: 'He settled everyone. It was important to our defence to know that they had a keeper who could take everything in the air.'

WEDNESDAY 6th NOVEMBER 1985

In relentless Macedonian rain, United turn in a professional performance to draw 1-1 against tough-tackling Vardar Skopje in the UEFA Cup. Paul Hegarty opens the scoring with his 12th ever goal in Europe, a header from an Eamonn Bannon cross after just 13 minutes, and 20-year-old future Red Star Belgrade, Inter and Yugoslavia star Darko Pančev equalises ten minutes later, but United stand firm. Maurice Malpas has to be carried off the pitch by his team-mates during the second half to receive stitches to a wound when the referee refuses to let the United physio come onto the pitch, but there are no more goals, and the Tangerines go through to the third round, 3-1 on aggregate.

SUNDAY 6th NOVEMBER 1983

Jim McLean spends three and a half hours at Ibrox to discuss becoming Rangers manager, ten days after John Greig resigned. The offer that Rangers make to McLean is financially the best any club ever offers him, and much more than United could afford to pay, and the Glasgow club also reassure McLean that he would be allowed to sign Catholic players. Following the meeting, neither McLean nor Rangers are giving anything away, but McLean has promised them an answer within 24 hours. One day earlier, four members of the United supporters' association spent 20 minutes with McLean to try to convince him to stay at Tannadice. Their spokesman, Finlay Mackay, says, 'We simply wanted to let him know our feelings. We pointed out that we are his family.'

SATURDAY 6th NOVEMBER 2010

David Goodwillie scores in his sixth consecutive league match, eight minutes after coming on as a second-half substitute, while 18-year-old Stuart Armstrong makes his United debut, as a late substitute, as United beat Hamilton 1-0.

MONDAY 7th NOVEMBER 1983

Although he is sorely tempted by the professional challenge of managing Rangers, Jim McLean lets his heart rule his head and lets loyalty trump ambition and financial gain, as he decides to stay at Tannadice. In gratitude, United announce that they'll arrange a testimonial match for him. McLean later reveals that, as well as Rangers, ten other clubs approached him about becoming their manager while he was at United, including Chelsea, Wolves, Hibs and Hearts.

WEDNESDAY 7th NOVEMBER 1973

United qualify for the semi-final of the Texaco Cup as they beat Leicester 1-0 at home and win 2-1 on aggregate. George Fleming opens the scoring in the 63rd minute when Leicester fail to clear a corner. Hamish McAlpine makes a good save from Len Glover ten minutes from the end as the Foxes throw everything at the Tangerines, but it's United who finish stronger, with Shilton having to save well from Tommy Traynor.

WEDNESDAY 7th NOVEMBER 1984

Although Dave Narey scores a remarkable own goal, United hammer Austrians Linz ASK 5-1 at home in the UEFA Cup. Paul Hegarty opens the scoring, before 21-year-old Tommy Coyne scores twice; 22-year-old Richard Gough blasts one home from 35 yards; and 20-year-old Dave Beaumont beats even that as he scores from 40 yards in the last minute.

WEDNESDAY 7th NOVEMBER 1990

United suffer their worst ever home defeat in Europe, as they lose 4-0 against Vitesse Arnhem at Tannadice and 5-0 on aggregate, bringing their 14-season run of consecutive European competition to an end. Jim McLean says: 'They were streets ahead of us. I am embarrassed first and foremost for Dundee United but also for Scottish football. People who ask why we buy foreign footballers saw the answer tonight.'

MONDAY 8th NOVEMBER 1999

Jerry Kerr dies at the age of 87. United say, 'He was an outstanding football club manager and a very kind and warm personality in the game. His record speaks for itself. He'll be remembered as the man who took Dundee United from the lower leagues of Scottish football to a position where the club was able to begin challenging for top honours on a regular basis.' Dundee FC say that Mr Kerr will be 'sorely missed by everyone involved in football in the city'.

SUNDAY 9th NOVEMBER 1997

United beat Aberdeen 5-0: their fifth consecutive win. Three of the goals come from Swedes Kjell Olofsson and Lars Zetterlund, who cracks a shot home from 30 yards, while Andy McLaren and Craig Easton get the others. Jim Leighton makes some great saves to keep the scoreline almost respectable. New United signing Mikael Andersson – who'd played against the Tangerines in a pre-season friendly – says, 'When I played against United in the summer they were training hard and played at half pace. I knew they could play better but I did not realise they could be this good.' Following the match, Aberdeen sack manager Roy Aitken.

SATURDAY 10th NOVEMBER 1928

United secure a bigger win than they have ever earned before, as they beat Stenhousemuir 8-0. Remarkably, star centre-forward Duncan Hutchison doesn't get any of the goals, although he plays well, sets quite a few up and almost scores several times. The first goal is an own goal, Harry Michie gets a hat-trick, Johnny Hart scores twice, and Jacky Kay and Dave Walker get one each. The result means that United have scored more goals in the season so far than any other league team in Scotland or England.

SATURDAY 10th NOVEMBER 1990

Duncan Ferguson makes his United debut, coming on as a substitute as the top-of-the-table Terrors beat Rangers 2-1 at Ibrox. But it's Darren Jackson, Alan Main and Maurice Malpas who make the headlines. Jackson grabs both goals, Main makes two particularly impressive saves, and Malpas – playing in central defence – doesn't put a foot wrong.

Maurice Malpas, Mr Reliable at Tannadice for 20 years and 830 games

SATURDAY 10th NOVEMBER 1962

Jerry Kerr's eyes light up 'as brightly as the new Tannadice lights', according to *The Evening Telegraph*, as United win their first home game played under floodlights, beating Rangers 2-1 in the league. The *Tele* says that 'Doug Smith had Jimmy Millar in his pocket; and full-backs Tommy Millar and Jimmy Briggs kept so close to international wingers Davie Wilson and Willie Henderson that the supply was cut off. Rangers had nobody to compare with United's forcing right-half and captain Tommy Neilson.' Wattie Carlyle opens the scoring with a thunderbolt from the edge of the box, before John Greig equalises and Jim Irvine gets the winner seven minutes from the end, as the Terrors' relentless pressure finally pays off. The *Tele* also notes that Jim Baxter was wearing suede winkle-pickers with light blue tongues, although presumably not during the match, and that one female Rangers fan sported an 'expensive-looking hat in club colours'.

THURSDAY 11th NOVEMBER 1971

After losing six of their first ten games of the season, United call their first ever press conference, where they announce that Jerry Kerr – Scotland's longest serving manager – is stepping down, after 12 almost entirely successful years in the job. Kerr had been taken ill at a recent match against Hibs, and the club say: 'We have been increasingly worried in recent weeks by the undue strain we have been placing on the manager, and it was no surprise when he intimated he wanted to resign. In order to lighten his burden, we have decided with his agreement to separate the administrative duties from the playing side. Accordingly, Mr Kerr will become general manager and an appointment will shortly be made of a team manager-coach.'

TUESDAY 12th NOVEMBER 1974

Twenty-year-old Hamilton striker Paul Hegarty signs for United, for a £40,000 fee that's higher than United have previously paid or Hamilton have previously received for a player. Accies manager Eric Smith says he's disgusted by Hegarty's 'unreasonable attitude', since the club didn't want to lose him but he made it clear that he wanted to move. But Smith does wish Hegarty well at Tannadice, and the move certainly does work out for the player and his new club.

SATURDAY 12th NOVEMBER 1983

Davie Dodds goes top of the Premier Division goalscoring charts, with 14 in all competitions for the season so far, as he grabs two in United's 7-0 defeat of St Johnstone. Dodds also wins a penalty, which Eamonn Bannon converts, while Paul Hegarty, Richard Gough and Billy Kirkwood all get on the scoresheet too, in a performance that Jim McLean describes as magnificent.

SATURDAY 13th NOVEMBER 1976

After almost exactly two years playing in attack for United, Paul Hegarty is played in defence, as an experiment, in a friendly away to Everton, which finishes 0-0. Hegarty is rarely out of United's defence for the next 13 years, eight of which he spends as captain.

SATURDAY 14th NOVEMBER 1942

The Sunday Post reports that there's a lot of zip but not much quality as United beat an RAF XI 3-1 in a wartime friendly, with a deflected shot from former Portsmouth and Fulham player Jimmy Easson, who's making his only appearance for United, and two 'smashing first timers' from Laurie Nevins.

SATURDAY 15th NOVEMBER 1941

Just three months after making his United debut, 21-year-old scoring sensation Albert Juliussen – who plays for United while he's stationed in Perth with the Black Watch – scores six in one game for United, and wins the penalty that provides their other goal, in a 7-1 defeat of St Bernard's, in the wartime North Eastern League Cup.

SATURDAY 16th NOVEMBER 1974

Paul Hegarty makes his United debut, coming on as a substitute for Andy Gray in a 5-0 away win over Partick Thistle, with the goals coming from Gray, Andy Rolland, Jackie Copland, Doug Houston and Dave Narey. *The Glasgow Herald* reports that United 'drew Thistle forward, built up their attacks patiently, lanced down the wings, and finished briskly', calls winger Iain McDonald a revelation, says that Jim McLean has 'worked wonders with men considered unusable at other clubs', labels Gray a prodigy and adds that young Narey can play a bit, too.

WEDNESDAY 16th NOVEMBER 1966

United's incredible start to their first ever season in Europe continues, as they beat Fairs Cup holders Barcelona for the second time in three weeks, 2-0 on a cold and windy Dundee night, in front of 28,000 fans, with the same line-up who won the away leg. After 18 minutes, Örjan Persson sets Ian Mitchell up to open the scoring. Persson comes close to getting a goal of his own twice before the break, Mitchell has another ruled out for offside, and in the second half Billy Hainey scores with a 30-yard shot to seal a famous and convincing victory. *The Glasgow Herald* describes the Terrors as stronger, quicker and more direct than their famous opponents, and says that any good ideas that the Catalan giants may have had are dealt with by the strength of United's tackling.

SATURDAY 17th NOVEMBER 1984

Paul Sturrock scores five in a 7-0 defeat of Morton, and then attributes his performance to the inspiration he's drawn from being part of the international squad as Scotland beat Spain 3-1 in a World Cup qualifier three days earlier. Jim McLean isn't there to see the demolition of Morton as he's away scouting Manchester United, with the two clubs due to meet in the UEFA Cup later in the month. Alex Taylor and Maurice Malpas get United's other goals, and Morton manager Willie McLean sums the match up when he says that his side 'were simply over-run', while *The Glasgow Herald* says that Sturrock 'found the time and space to educate everyone in the art of putting the ball into the back of the net'.

SATURDAY 18th NOVEMBER 1933

After losing ten of their first 14 league games of the season, United thrash Edinburgh City, 9-3 in front of just 200 fans in terrible weather at Tannadice. *The Evening Telegraph* reports that the visitors' defence 'floundered in the mud' while 'the Tannadice sharpshooters made merry', with Willie Ouchterlonie scoring five. But in spite of the scoreline, the *Tele* criticises United's left wing, saying that Harry Nicolson is rarely seen and that Laurie McBain – who scores twice – fails to live up to his potential. Both players soon leave the club.

WEDNESDAY 19th NOVEMBER 1980

In cold November rain, United beat Celtic 3-0 in the League Cup semi-final away leg, to win 4-1 on aggregate and set up a final against Dundee. The goals come from Willie Pettigrew, Paul Sturrock and Davie Dodds, in what Jim McLean calls 'the greatest team effort since I've been manager', while Celtic boss Billy McNeill says United are 'magnificent in all ways'.

SATURDAY 19th NOVEMBER 1960

Former Celtic star and Scotland international Neil Mochan scores twice on his debut for United, at the age of 33. The veteran striker goes on to score 35 goals in 85 appearances for the Terrors.

SATURDAY 19th NOVEMBER 1994

Robbie Winters makes his debut for United as a substitute, but it's Christian Dailly who's the star of the show in a 5-2 defeat of Hearts, a high point in a difficult season. The Edinburgh side take an early lead but, one minute later, Grant Johnson cracks the Tangerines' equaliser into the net from the edge of the box. Craig Brewster heads home from a corner ten minutes later and it's 3-1 to United just 18 minutes into the match, as Billy McKinlay receives a pass from Dailly and blasts the ball past Henry Smith from pretty much exactly the same spot as Johnson. Twenty minutes later a long McKinlay pass sets up Dailly, who creates space for himself to fire home, again from the edge of the box. In the second half, a Dailly header from a Maurice Malpas cross makes it 5-1, before Hearts get a consolation goal from the rebound after a soft penalty. Manager Ivan Golac says, 'We were caught napping at the first goal, but came back to play football of the highest order and score some beautiful goals.'

SATURDAY 20th NOVEMBER 1937

Duncan Hutchison scores twice in the first five minutes as United demolish East Stirling 6-1. Albert Robinson scores either side of the break, before Hutchison sets up his younger brother Dan to stretch the lead with a header, and Dennis McGurk, who's only at Tannadice for a few weeks, gets United's sixth.

WEDNESDAY 21st NOVEMBER 1973

Dave Narey makes his United debut in a 2-1 defeat of Falkirk, in front of just 1,250 fans, in a re-arranged league match that takes place on a Wednesday afternoon, because of government restrictions on the use of floodlights during the miners' strike. Narey – one of three 17-year-olds in the side – plays well but is perhaps fortunate not to give away a penalty when he gets close to Kirkie Lawson in the first half. Very soon he's firmly established as a first pick, at the start of a long and glittering United career.

SATURDAY 21st NOVEMBER 1925

The first ever top-flight Dundee derby finishes 0-0, with the match's highlight coming when United goalie Bill Paterson leaps to tip a Napper Thomson penalty over the bar. The size of the crowd – estimated to be at least 16,000 – seems to take the Dens Park officials by surprise, as there's a delay getting them into the ground as extra turnstiles have to be opened. *The Evening Telegraph* credits United with 'a meritorious performance indeed' to earn a draw, saying that 'quite a number did not expect it, but nevertheless United managed it. And, what's more, they were worth it.'

SATURDAY 21st NOVEMBER 1981

Maurice Malpas makes his United debut, at the age of 19, in a 4-0 defeat of Airdrie. Mattieu Bollen – the coach of Belgian side Winterslag, United's upcoming UEFA Cup opponents, who's on a scouting mission at the match – says that United 'are better than Arsenal [who Winterslag beat in the previous round]. They seem to score goals with their eyes shut.' Malpas, meanwhile, goes on to play 830 times for United, captains the side that wins the Scottish Cup for the first ever time, and earns two testimonial matches before eventually becoming assistant manager.

SUNDAY 22nd NOVEMBER 1981

The fouls and the yellow cards fly in Belgium as Jim McLean watches United's UEFA Cup opponents Winterslag in action in Antwerp. Winterslag goalie Roger de Bruyne is sent off for a nasty foul and the police move in to stop trouble on the terraces, as bottles are thrown.

SATURDAY 23rd NOVEMBER 2013

Seventeen-year-old Ryan Gauld's precise passes set up all four goals as the Tangerines beat Partick Thistle 4-1 at Tannadice. Gary Mackay-Steven scores twice, with his first coming in the second minute, teenager Andy Robertson gets one, and substitute Brian Graham completes the scoring, with his first goal for the club. The result puts United fourth in the league.

WEDNESDAY 24th NOVEMBER 1982

At a muddy Tannadice, United beat Werder Bremen in the first leg of their UEFA Cup third-round tie. The Tangerines open the scoring after 15 minutes, when Davie Dodds and Eamonn Bannon play a neat one-two and Bannon sets up Ralph Milne to turn the ball into the net. But it all gets a bit nervous after that, with 22-year-old Rudi Völler in particular spurning two great chances to score for the visitors. The equaliser does come though, when Norbert Meier knocks home the rebound from a Völler shot in the second half, before, near the end, Milne turns provider, for Dave Narey, whose chip makes it 2-1, to leave the tie finely balanced going into the second leg.

SATURDAY 24th NOVEMBER 1979

In torrential rain at neutral East End Park, United thrash Hamilton 6-2 in the League Cup semi-final. The score's only 2-1 at half-time but the floodgates open after the break. With Arabs outnumbering their rivals by four to one in the stands, Paul Sturrock runs the show, scoring two and setting up the others, with Billy Kirkwood getting a couple and Willie Pettigrew and Paul Hegarty one each, as the club march convincingly on to the final two weeks later, against Aberdeen.

WEDNESDAY 25th NOVEMBER 1959

Teenager Jim Irvine gets a hat-trick as United beat Arbroath 7-3 at home in the Forfarshire Cup. Tommy Neilson, Dennis Gillespie, Jim Stalker and Jim Bell all get on the scoresheet too, as *The Evening Telegraph* reports that the United forwards cut through the Arbroath defence at will, with the goals coming from fine understanding and teamwork, securing a result that sends the Red Lichties secretary, trainer and coach 'into the depths of depression'.

WEDNESDAY 26th NOVEMBER 1986

Paul Sturrock sets up both of United's goals as they beat Hajduk Split 2-0 at home in the UEFA Cup third round first leg. Jim McInally gets his first for the club, and John Clark – who threatens Hajduk's goal regularly throughout – scores the second, to give the Tangerines a healthy lead ahead of the tricky away match.

THURSDAY 27th NOVEMBER 1975

Full-back Andy Rolland, who has been at Tannadice for ten years and made hundreds of appearances for United, is suspended by the club for moving to Glenrothes, under Jim McLean's strict rules about players having to live in Dundee. Rolland has accepted the offer of a council house in his native Fife, after being on the waiting list for three years while living in Whitfield. He says, 'We have never really liked living in the area and my wife, who has been ill recently, is expecting our third child. I must make this move into a better environment for the sake of my family.' Rolland returns to the team three weeks later.

WEDNESDAY 28th NOVEMBER 1934

Nineteen-year-old Arthur Milne scores four on his United debut, a 15-goal thriller against Edinburgh City at a muddy Tannadice. Unfortunately, with the game played on a Wednesday afternoon to avoid a clash with Dundee's home fixture with Hibs in the evening, only 1,600 fans see the remarkable match, which *The Courier* describes as 'serious drama in its first phase' and 'pantomime in its second'. The visitors take a shock 4-1 lead, but United draw level by half-time, then score five more in a row before City get two consolation goals, making the final score 9-6 to United. George Ross and Alec King score twice each for the home side, while Jimmy Smith gets one and also misses a penalty. *The Courier* calls Milne a nippy raider and a lad with plenty of pluck. He sustains an injury when he scores his first goal, but recovers to score twice with headers before rifling home his fourth from 30 yards. Meanwhile, Brechin City aren't happy. They say Milne signed for them before he joined United, but the SFA reject their appeal, and he goes on to score 109 goals for United.

SATURDAY 28th NOVEMBER 1981

United narrowly miss out on becoming just the second Scottish club to win three consecutive League Cups, when they controversially lose the final 2-1 to Rangers. A typically excellent Paul Sturrock pass and a characteristically explosive run and shot from Ralph Milne – who received a more-than-stern half-time dressing-down from Jim McLean for not doing that sort of thing in the first half – add up to a 47th-minute lead for the Tannadice men, and Sturrock cracks the ball into the net from 20 yards eight minutes later, but John Holt is deemed to be interfering with play and is flagged offside. Rangers score with two late free kicks as United are denied the trophy. McLean is careful with his post-match comments about the key offside decision, saying 'there are excuses for our defeat if people want to make them'.

WEDNESDAY 28th NOVEMBER 1984

Jim McLean perhaps seems optimistic ahead of the first leg of United's UEFA Cup third-round tie, away to Manchester United, when he says 'a score draw would do us', but that's exactly what his team give him, in what is – especially in the second half – one of their best performances in their many European matches. Manchester United attack relentlessly in the first half, but Hegarty, Narey, Gough, Malpas and McAlpine defend resolutely, with the big keeper saving a Gordon Strachan penalty. Strachan scores from another spot kick to give the home side a 1-0 lead, but, after the break, the Terrors are full of confidence, and Hegarty and Sturrock each score, either side of a Bryan Robson goal, to send 5,000 Arabs back up the motorway very happy indeed.

WEDNESDAY 29th NOVEMBER 1978

Dave Narey plays in his first full competitive match for Scotland, playing the whole 90 minutes in a European Championship qualifier against Portugal, in Lisbon, under Jock Stein. For once Lisbon isn't a happy hunting ground for Stein though, with Narey and his team-mates struggling to control their talented opponents, who win 1-0. Nevertheless, United celebrate Narey's milestone by flying the Lion Rampant at Tannadice, but have to take it down because the Lion Rampant is the property of the sovereign and can only be flown in the presence of royalty.

SUNDAY 30th NOVEMBER 1997

United lose the League Cup Final to Celtic, 3-0 at Ibrox, while Hampden is being redeveloped. Celtic's third goal has more than a hint of offside against it, and Kjell Olofsson comes close to pulling one back with a fierce 25-yard free kick early in the second half, but the disappointing truth is that Wim Jansen's Celtic side – who are on their way to winning the league for the first time in 10 years – are the better team on the day.

DUNDEE UNITED

ON THIS DAY

DECEMBER

TUESDAY 1st DECEMBER 1981

On a terrible muddy playing surface in Belgium, United secure a goalless draw in the first leg of their UEFA Cup tie against Winterslag. The Swiss referee gives the game the go-ahead even though the pitch has been turned to mud by heavy rain and there are large amounts of surface water, and, half an hour before kick-off, it's churned up more by a marching band, whom the match officials desperately try to wave off of the pitch. Jim McLean calls the decision to play the match a 'farce' and United make an official complaint to UEFA, but it doesn't matter in the end as the Tangerines are in the driving seat at full time, following typically commanding and composed performances from Paul Hegarty and Dave Narey, and after Paul Sturrock and Eamonn Bannon have forced several good saves from Belgian keeper Jean-Paul de Bruyne.

SATURDAY 1st DECEMBER 1956

Johnny Coyle scores four as United beat Albion Rovers 7-0, taking his record for the season to 26 goals after 23 games, six goals ahead of his nearest rival at the top of the Second Division goalscoring chart. United's other goals are scored by Maurice Milne and wingers Don Watt – with his first for the club – and Jimmy Forbes – with his last for the club.

SATURDAY 2nd DECEMBER 1995

Craig Brewster scores four as United – who are playing in their third choice strip for the first time – record their biggest win since 1967, beating Dumbarton 8-0. *The Evening Telegraph* describes the Terrors' performance as sensational, Robbie Winters as rampant, and Dumbarton defender Martin Melvin's headed own goal as cracking, and says that the score could have been higher if Owen Coyle hadn't 'forgotten where the goal was for most of the game'. Coyle does score one though, as do Grant Johnson and Gary McSwegan, while Maurice Malpas hits the bar. The massive score comes in spite of the visitors playing with five men in defence, and Sons boss Jim Fallon says 'I've never experienced anything like that', while Brewster says, 'This will give us a lift and put confidence through the team.' The win helps to ease the pain of a shock defeat against the same opposition in October.

FRIDAY 3rd DECEMBER 1971

After being directly approached by the Tannadice directors, Dundee coach Jim McLean is appointed as Dundee United manager, at the age of 34, while Jerry Kerr becomes general manager and club secretary. McLean says: 'I am delighted. I have full control of the team and everything connected with selection. I must point out that this has nothing to do with the appointment of Davie White as manager of Dundee.' But McLean later admits that he would have been unable to work with new Dundee boss White, and that he had sounded out Jerry Kerr about becoming a coach at Tannadice, shortly before being offered the manager job. And McLean also later reveals that he was very worried and nervous about stepping up to management and would have been happier to remain a coach. Oblivious to McLean's self-doubt, *The Glasgow Herald* predicts that, 'His tactical knowledge could make the Tannadice team into one of the most potent forces in Scottish football.' It's a prescient comment but even its writer would likely end up surprised by exactly how accurate it is.

SATURDAY 4th DECEMBER 1971

Jerry Kerr picks the United team for the last time, as the Tangerines lose 3-2 away to Hearts, with United's goals coming from Alan Gordon and Tommy Traynor. New manager Jim McLean says 'the potential is there but I was disappointed in the matter of all-round effort', and immediately orders extra training sessions.

SATURDAY 5th DECEMBER 1964

United are struggling at the bottom of the First Division as their first foreign players, Swede Örjan Persson and Dane Finn Døssing, make their debuts, away to Hearts, three days after signing at Tannadice. Dunfermline, St Johnstone and Morton were also interested in signing skilful midfielder Persson, who initially has to play as an amateur because of Swedish FA rules. Døssing, who'd scored 43 goals in the previous season for his club, Viborg, and who scored four times in a trial match for United, scores the Terrors' only goal at Tynecastle, as they lose 3-1. But it's onwards and upwards after that for United with their Scandinavian recruits, as Lennart Wing and Mogens Berg follow Persson and Døssing to Tayside, with great success.

SATURDAY 6th DECEMBER 1980

For the second successive season, United win the League Cup at Dens Park, beating Dundee in the final, in front of a capacity crowd, on a cold day on a pitch covered in frost and patches of snow. The final is goalless until the stroke of half-time, when Paul Sturrock twists away from two defenders out on the left and chips the ball across the box to onrushing Davie Dodds, who heads home the opener. In the second half Sturrock scores twice, each one almost a carbon copy of the other as he knocks home rebounds from Paul Hegarty headers following corners, to seal a comprehensive win and clear the way for a beaming Hamish McAlpine to lift the trophy. Jim McLean says he couldn't be more pleased and that the team have played some marvellous football throughout the competition.

SATURDAY 7th DECEMBER 1974

In his third appearance as a substitute for United, 20-year-old Paul Hegarty scores his first goal for the club, in a 3-3 draw with Clyde. The Tangerines are 3-1 down with five minutes to go, when Jackie Copland pulls one back and then Hegarty gets the equaliser one minute later. Although striker Hegarty soon moves into defence, he goes on to score 81 more goals for United.

SATURDAY 8th DECEMBER 1979

Because of flooding and heavy traffic, United arrive at Hampden just 30 minutes before the League Cup Final against Aberdeen, which ends goalless after extra time in bad weather, as both sides create chances but the defences are on top. Following the match, it's announced over the Hampden tannoy that the replay will take place at Hampden too, but league secretary Jim Farry later says 'after strong representations from both Aberdeen and Dundee United in favour of Dens Park, the committee have decided to accede to the clubs' request [to change the venue for the replay].' It's the first time that the League Cup Final will be played away from Hampden. Meanwhile, Jim McLean says: 'I feel that Aberdeen played as well as they could but they still didn't manage to beat us. We were short of our best, but we can improve on Wednesday.'

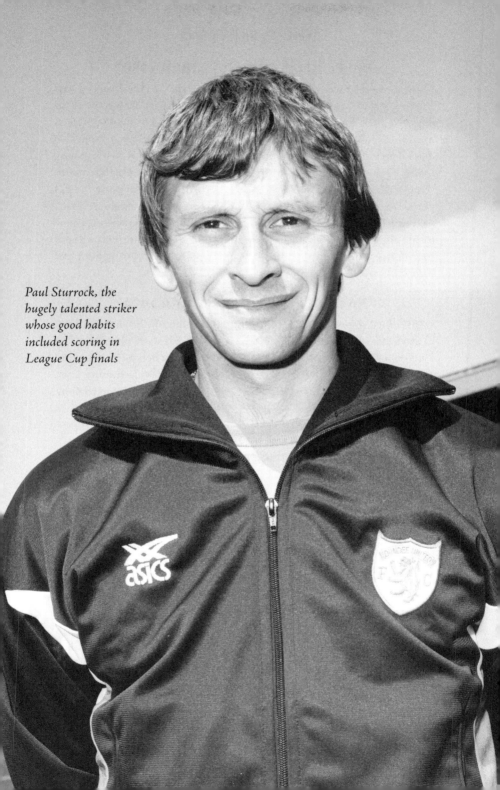

Paul Sturrock, the hugely talented striker whose good habits included scoring in League Cup finals

WEDNESDAY 8th DECEMBER 1982

In the third round of the UEFA Cup, United draw 1-1 away against Werder Bremen, and win 3-2 on aggregate. Paul Hegarty gets the night off to a brilliant start, heading home an away goal from a Ralph Milne corner in the third minute, but, after Rudi Völler equalises in the third minute of the second half, it's backs to the wall for the rest of the match. Hegarty and Dave Narey are immense at the back – although Völler hits the bar twice and the post once – and the Tangerines survive a relentless onslaught to become the only British side in the quarter-finals. Jim McLean says: 'I'm very proud for Scottish football, and we felt that responsibility tonight. I wasn't happy at all about all that pressure in the second half but I have to remember that Werder were lucky to get away with a 2-1 scoreline at Tannadice.'

SATURDAY 9th DECEMBER 1978

United, who are sitting at the top of the Premier Division, beat Rangers by a wider margin than they've ever beaten them before, 3-0. *The Evening Telegraph* says: 'How full of everything that's best in the game was the United mixture that practically reduced the Light Blues to frenzied impotence.' The Terrors excel in every department, as Davie Dodds opens the scoring in three minutes, before George Fleming doubles the score with a cracking effort 18 minutes later, and Dave Narey nonchalantly plays keepy-uppy while he waits to take a second-half penalty that he then scores, to seal the handsome victory.

WEDNESDAY 9th DECEMBER 1981

United reach the UEFA Cup quarter-finals for the first time, as they win 5-0 at home against a Winterslag team who almost all wear tights to cope with a particularly cold December evening in Dundee. Maurice Malpas, playing his first game in Europe, almost opens the scoring after 17 minutes when his shot is blocked and he knocks the rebound narrowly wide. But, within 20 minutes of that, the Terrors are 3-0 up, through Eamonn Bannon, Dave Narey and then Paul Hegarty, and a second-half Ralph Milne double seals a commanding victory. It's United's last home game for two months because the winter's so cold.

WEDNESDAY 10th DECEMBER 1986

Hajduk Split rattle the woodwork twice but United earn a goalless draw away in the UEFA Cup third round second leg, to win 2-0 on aggregate. United, who are missing Paul Hegarty, Maurice Malpas and Paul Sturrock to injury, have to work hard, particularly in defence – where Gary McGinnis proves an accomplished stand-in for Hegarty – against talented opponents, but do enough to earn their place in the quarter-finals, where they will face Barcelona.

SATURDAY 11th DECEMBER 1982

Jim McLean, who's concerned about the recent form of Davie Dodds and Paul Sturrock, plays 20-year-old John Reilly up front against Kilmarnock, with Dodds on the bench. Reilly repays his manager's faith with two goals, and Dodds also scores twice, after coming on as a second-half substitute, in a 7-0 victory that also includes a goal apiece for Eamonn Bannon, Dave Narey – with a sweet 20-yard strike – and Ralph Milne, who gets the biggest cheer of a happy afternoon when he bursts forward from inside his own half, beats four men and slots the ball home for goal number five, with a cast-iron contender for goal of the season. And although Sturrock doesn't score, McLean says that his contribution makes it 'his top performance for weeks – if not the season'.

SATURDAY 11th DECEMBER 1993

Ivan Golac promises to beat Rangers by three or four goals and he delivers on that promise as his United side turn in an excellent performance at Ibrox to comprehensively defeat the champions 3-0. All of the goals come early in the first half, from Dave Bowman in the first minute, Paddy Connolly after a quarter of an hour, and Craig Brewster six minutes after that. Rangers defenders Dave McPherson and Richard Gough are both substituted between the second and third goals, although manager Walter Smith says it's because they're injured, rather than because of the torrid time the Terrors are giving them. Golac says 'Our players were magnificent – I wouldn't give any of them less than nine out of ten.' He praises Connolly and Brewster for defending from the front, while Brian Welsh, Gordan Petrić and Freddy van der Hoorn don't give Mark Hateley or Gordon Durie a look-in at the other end.

SATURDAY 11th DECEMBER 1971

Jim McLean's first game in charge of United is an underwhelming draw at home against Ayr United. The Tangerines take the lead twice, through Kenny Cameron and Tommy Traynor, but twice the Honest Men equalise, as the United players seem to tire late on, amid suggestions that McLean's extra training and confusion caused by his new tactics are having a negative impact. The new boss's verdict is 'not good enough' and his solution is more training, and team changes. His methods are eventually proved right.

WEDNESDAY 12th DECEMBER 1979

On a wet and windy night at Dens Park, United earn their first ever major honour, as they dominate the League Cup Final replay against Aberdeen. Willie Pettigrew scores twice, before Paul Sturrock beats the offside trap and races 40 yards to make it 3-0, sending the Arabs in the capacity crowd – which is higher at Dens Park than it was for the original match at Hampden – wild with joy. In the Tannadice boardroom a few hours later, United director Ernie Robertson has tears in his eyes as he tells Jim McLean he never thought he'd see the club win a major honour. The next day, McLean says, 'I have watched this side grow up and I have been as severe a critic – maybe more so – than anyone else. But I must say that they got it as near perfect as I would want it.' With a characteristic combination of ambition and doubt, he adds: 'We will get better but it's easier to become a good side than to stay one.'

WEDNESDAY 12th DECEMBER 1984

On a dramatic, heart-breaking night at a packed Tannadice, Dundee United lose 3-2 to Manchester United in the UEFA Cup. Mark Hughes opens the scoring when Dave Narey can't clear a Gordon Strachan cross, then a Richard Gough shot is cleared off the line, and Paul Sturrock sets Davie Dodds up for the equaliser, before unlucky Tangerines defender Gary McGinnis heads a corner into his own net. In the second half, the Terrors equalise for the fourth time in the tie, through a towering Paul Hegarty header, before a deflected Arnold Mühren shot seals a 5-4 aggregate victory for the men from Old Trafford.

WEDNESDAY 12th DECEMBER 1973

Newcastle visit Tannadice for the first leg of the Texaco Cup semi-final, and the Tangerines throw everything at the Magpies throughout the first half, firing in more than a dozen shots and scoring twice in the first 20 minutes, with Frank Kopel turning home a Tommy Traynor corner, and Archie Knox volleying a rebound into the net after Newcastle goalie Willie McFaul parries an Andy Gray shot. McFaul makes impressive saves throughout the match, while the visitors improve after the break, and there are no more goals, although Pat Gardner rattles the crossbar from 25 yards. With a decent amount of sponsorship money in the tournament destined for players' pockets, Ian Archer in *The Glasgow Herald* says that if the United players 'fell short of playing as if their lives depended upon the result, they showed enough aggression to suggest that their mortgages and Majorcan holidays were at least involved', as they secure their well-deserved comprehensive first-leg lead.

TUESDAY 13th DECEMBER 1983

United's Davie Dodds makes his Scotland debut in a home international against Northern Ireland. The Scots lose 2-0 to goals from Norman Whiteside and Sammy McIlroy, and Dodds never plays for Scotland again.

SATURDAY 14th DECEMBER 1974

Teenagers Dave Narey and Andy Gray are dominating all the headlines as an impressive run of United form – during which the Terrors score a total of 20 goals in five consecutive league games – culminates in a 6-0 away defeat of Morton, with Narey opening the scoring in the third minute, Paul Hegarty and Gray getting two each and Frank Kopel sealing the victory with a penalty near the end.

SATURDAY 15th DECEMBER 1934

Two weeks after beating Edinburgh City 9-6 at home, free-scoring United visit the capital and win the reverse fixture 8-2, in front of just 85 fans. *The Evening Telegraph* credits United with 'snappy football', and says that they're so dominant that goalie Peter Robertson has little else to do but shiver in the cold and rain. Alec King grabs a hat-trick while George Ross and Arthur Milne get two goals each and Bobby Gardiner scores once.

SATURDAY 16th DECEMBER 1933

'If football drama were written and not played, no dramatist could have conceived more thrilling denouement' says 'The Laird' in *The Courier*. The subjects of his amazement are a remarkable comeback from United and a bizarre refereeing decision that almost robs them of the chance to complete that turnaround. Ten-man United, who have lost captain Laurie MacBain to a broken leg in the first half, are 4-1 down against Arbroath after 75 minutes, when two quick goals from George Ross and Jim 'Monty' Munro make it 4-3, and, straight after Munro's goal, referee Mr Allan blows for full time. But there are still nine minutes left to play, impassioned protests are made and Mr Allan admits his mistake and restarts the match – once he's caught up with the Red Lichties goalie, who's already halfway to the dressing room. Five minutes later, debutant Bobby Gardiner crashes the equaliser into the net from the edge of the box, as, says The Laird, the crowd go into ecstacies.

SATURDAY 17th DECEMBER 2016

Despite playing 35 minutes with ten men after defender Lewis Toshney is shown a second yellow card, United secure their sixth consecutive clean sheet, in a 0-0 draw away to Raith Rovers. The Tangerines have a chance to take all three points when they win a penalty 15 minutes from the end, but Raith goalie Kevin Cuthbert saves well from Tony Andreu. The result leaves United level on points with Hibs at the top of the Championship. Manager Ray McKinnon says: 'To get a point against a tough team like Raith with just ten men was absolutely outstanding and if you had said to us three months ago we would be up at the top of the league we would have taken that.'

SATURDAY 18th DECEMBER 1982

Midway through the 1982/83 league title race, United get an important win in difficult conditions, 2-1 away against Morton on a pitch covered in hard-packed snow. The home side open the scoring early on but John Reilly equalises with an overhead kick before, in the second half, Eamonn Bannon chases down a pass that seems too far ahead of him, and crosses to Paul Sturrock, who seals the victory.

SATURDAY 19th DECEMBER 1914

On a frosty Tannadice pitch, Collie Martin scores five in a 6-1 defeat of Albion Rovers. Martin – who finishes top scorer in both of the seasons that he spends with Dundee Hibs before his football career is cut short by World War I – is in 'irresistible form' according to *The Courier*. Tragically, Martin is killed in 1915 near Ypres, where he's serving as a corporal with the Black Watch.

SATURDAY 19th DECEMBER 1925

In their first season in Division One, United come from behind to beat Rangers in frost and snow at Tannadice. Rangers lead, through a controversial penalty, at half-time, but Micky Campbell and Tommy Simpson strike in the second half, while – according to *The Courier* – the United defence is as sound as the Bank of England. *The Courier* also says, 'The way that the Tannadice lads knocked the stuffing out of the Light Blues was an exhilarating example of what can be done on great occasions,' and that the match 'will be written in capital letters on the history sheets of the league youngsters.'

WEDNESDAY 19th DECEMBER 1973

Leading 2-0 from the home leg of their Texaco Cup semi-final against Newcastle, Dundee United lose an early goal in the away leg, but Andy Gray equalises after six minutes. Late in the first half, Hamish McAlpine saves a penalty, but Newcastle bring on Malcolm Macdonald – who's returning from seven weeks out injured – and pull one back before Macdonald levels the tie on aggregate with ten minutes to go. With no away goals rule in the Texaco Cup, the match goes to extra time. United force two good saves from Willie McFaul, before Newcastle's Tommy Cassidy gets the winner to send the Tangerines out, 4-3 on aggregate.

TUESDAY 20th DECEMBER 1988

Jim McLean becomes United chairman, and immediately announces that he hopes to find someone to replace him as manager 'in the foreseeable future', since he can no longer spend as much time with the players as he thinks he should. But he manages to perform both roles for a few years, before the club finds his successor.

SATURDAY 20th DECEMBER 1986

Hearts are leading United 1-0 at Tannadice with ten minutes to go, when the Tangerines pull off a stunning comeback. Jim McInally pokes the ball through to Paul Sturrock, who turns it past Henry Smith for the equaliser, and just two minutes later Eamonn Bannon bursts forward and blasts the ball across Smith into the corner. The final goal is the pick of the bunch, as Iain Ferguson robs Sandy Jardine 40 yards out and immediately lobs the Hearts keeper. Archie MacPherson describes the match's climax – and Bannon and Ferguson's goals – as some of the best football he's seen in the season so far.

SATURDAY 21st DECEMBER 1985

Alex Ferguson is sent to the stand as United beat league champions Aberdeen 2-1 at Tannadice. *The Glasgow Herald* says that United play with more style than they did in their league title-winning season, as Jim McLean takes a risk on Paul Sturrock, who's nursing a hamstring problem, and it pays off handsomely. Sturrock is involved as United win an early penalty, which Eamonn Bannon converts, and the skinny striker scores the second, as the Tangerines stretch their unbeaten run to seven matches, in an exciting title race.

SATURDAY 22nd DECEMBER 1934

'Crazy Stuff at Tannadice' is the headline in *The Courier*, as Arthur Milne scores four, George Ross gets three and Dave Corbett and Jimmy Smith strike once each – while Willie MacRitchie has a penalty saved – as United thrash Brechin 9-2, two months after beating them 8-0 away. Milne's efforts take his total to 11 goals in four games, and Smith's goal is the pick of the bunch, as he dribbles through the visitors' defence, past the keeper and into the net.

SATURDAY 23rd DECEMBER 1972

Two days before Christmas, Jim McLean hands out free chocolate to children and pensioners at United's home match against Dumbarton. Unfortunately, Stuart Markland and Hamish McAlpine dish out gifts too, each giving an own goal to the visitors, who are 2-1 up at half-time. But an Andy Rolland equaliser and a Doug Smith penalty earn United full points for Christmas.

SATURDAY 24th DECEMBER 1927

Duncan 'Hurricane' Hutchison scores twice on his debut, away to Bathgate, as United come from behind to win 2-1.

THURSDAY 25th DECEMBER 1924

United go top of Division Two as they beat Stenhousemuir 3-0 at Tannadice, with a first-half goal from Tommy Simpson and a second-half double from William Mackie, while Bobby Bauld misses a penalty. United go on to win the league and earn promotion for the first time.

SATURDAY 25th DECEMBER 1926

At Christmas Carroll is the main man in United's 2-0 defeat of Rangers at Tannadice. A header from Eddie Carroll hits the bar on the stroke of half-time, and Jock McDonald rushes in to head home the rebound. And ten minutes into the second half, Carroll makes it 2-0, when he races onto a Willie Welsh pass and fires the ball high into the net. *The Courier* calls United's victory 'spanking' and praises the performances of the whole team. It will be more than 50 years before they beat the Glasgow side by a wider margin.

SATURDAY 25th DECEMBER 1909

On Dundee Hibs' first Christmas Day, Dundee Wanderers visit an icy Tannadice in the Carrie Cup, a league tournament that also includes Brechin, Forfar, Arbroath and Montrose, and which Hibs go on to win, as their first trophy. Hibs don't give Wanderers any gifts as they go 5-1 up at half-time and end up winning 6-2, with Henny Brown, Tim Dailly, Peter Yule and Archibald Downie among the goalscorers.

TUESDAY 25th DECEMBER 1956

In the only match played in the Scottish Second Division on Christmas Day 1956, United put six goals past Berwick Rangers for the second time in three months, with five of the goals coming in one 30-minute spell in the second half. Milne and Sturrock are on the scoresheet, but they're Maurice and Dave rather than Ralph and Paul, and United's other goals come from Don Watt, Johnny Coyle and a Jimmy Reid double.

SATURDAY 26th DECEMBER 1959

Dave Whytock scores a debut hat-trick, in United's sixth consecutive league win, a 6-0 defeat of East Fife. Dennis Gillespie scores two and Jim Irvine gets the other, as *The Evening Telegraph* says: 'There's urgency, fighting spirit and no little craft in a [United] team that contains a handful of outstanding members in [Tommy] Graham, [Tommy] Neilson, [Ron] Yeats, Gillespie and Irvine, with newcomer Whytock looking as if he will soon join the select band. There's red hot enthusiasm on the terracings, with much volume added to the famous roar by the amplifying qualities of the covered enclosure.' The *Tele* also says that the fans' hopes of promotion are not misplaced. Whytock's Tannadice career doesn't develop as hoped, unfortunately – he only makes eight more appearances for United – but the Terrors do earn promotion at the end of the season.

SATURDAY 27th DECEMBER 1941

United beat a Polish Army XI, 3-0, in a wartime friendly at Tannadice. With Albert Juliussen unable to play, Ian Smart, Bobby Gardiner and Sid Smith score for the home side. In *The Evening Telegraph*, 'Rambler' laments the Poles' reluctance to take on opponents instead of constantly passing the ball, but acknowledges that the game is entertaining.

SATURDAY 27th DECEMBER 1980

Teenager Ralph Milne – who's playing from the start in a league game for the first time since August – is repeatedly booed by his own side's fans for missing chances in a home match against Hearts, then scores twice as United win 4-1. Jim McLean says: 'Never before have I been so ashamed. The youngster did miss chances, true, but the harder those on the terracings called for his replacement, the more determined I became that he was staying where he was.' Meanwhile, *The Glasgow Herald* describes United's performance in the match as evidence of their transformation from possible relegation candidates to outside title challengers.

SATURDAY 28th DECEMBER 1963

Ian Mitchell gets a hat-trick as United – playing in black – thump St Mirren 6-2, with five of their goals coming in the second half, and Dennis Gillespie, Jim Irvine and Jimmy McManus scoring once each.

SATURDAY 28th DECEMBER 1935

The name Milne is on the scoresheet six times in one match as Arthur Milne scores four and Johnny Milne gets two in an 8-0 defeat of Dumbarton. Jimmy Smith opens the scoring, before the Milne floodgates open, and Robert Murray scores his only ever goal for United. *The Evening Telegraph* says that the Sons' goalkeeper McIntyre 'performed nobly in face of the tornado, and but for his brilliance – and the woodwork – there is no doubt that Tranmere's total of 13 last week [the Merseyside club beat Oldham 13-4 on Christmas Day] would have been put in the shade.'

SATURDAY 29th DECEMBER 1973

On a day overshadowed by sadness as great United manager Jimmy Brownlie dies at the age of 88, 18-year-old Andy Gray scores four and misses a penalty as United beat Dumbarton 6-0. *The Evening Telegraph* are impressed by Gray, but question the widespread £150,000 valuation of 'a laddie so recently come to the front'.

SATURDAY 29th DECEMBER 1928

League leaders United beat Bathgate 6-1, but the result – and United's 4-0 away defeat of the same team earlier in the season – are expunged when Bathgate resign from the league. Unfortunately Bathgate's withdrawal means that United finish the season with 99 league goals, rather than 109, although they still win the league and get promoted.

SATURDAY 30th DECEMBER 1967

United beat Stirling Albion 9-0, with the ninth goal the pick of the bunch, as Ian Mitchell capitalises on an excellent long pass from Dennis Gillespie. *The Evening Telegraph* says, 'And what a pass it was. A searching, searing, 50-yard straight-upfield offering that sizzled as it skimmed the turf. Seemingly, magically, to apply its own brakes as it sped close past already-on-the-move Mitchell. No need for Mitchell to break stride. He ran on to take over control, closed in on goal – and delivered the perfect answer to those who say it don't mean a thing if it ain't got the big build-up. It even warmed the chilled hearts and bodies of the reporters up in the press-box that becomes an ice-box when the polar winds do blow.'

SATURDAY 31st DECEMBER 1966

For the first of two times in Celtic's quadruple-winning season, United beat Jock Stein's men, 3-2. Twice the Terrors come from behind at Tannadice, first through Finn Døssing and then – after Døssing and Örjan Persson switch wings in the second half and the Terrors take control – through a 25-yard Dennis Gillespie strike, before Ian Mitchell takes the ball past Celtic goalie Ronnie Simpson and rolls the winner into the net, 15 minutes from the end. United are the only Scottish team to beat Celtic during the season.

Also available at all good book stores

9781785314391

9781785311802

9781905411832

9781909178847

9781848182004

9781785314384